Gathering

Published by 404 Ink
www.404Ink.com
@404Ink

First published in Great Britain, 2024

Editing: Durre Shahwar & Nasia Sarwar-Skuse
Illustrations: Haricha Abdaal
Typesetting: Laura Jones-Rivera
Proofreading: Laura Jones-Rivera
Cover design: Holly Ovenden
Co-founders and publishers of 404 Ink:
Heather McDaid & Laura Jones-Rivera

Print ISBN: 9781912489749
Ebook ISBN: 9781912489756

Printed and bound in Great Britain by Clays Ltd, Elcograf S.p.A.

404 Ink acknowledges and is thankful for the financial support of
Books Council of Wales and Creative Scotland
in the publication of this title.

CYNGOR LLYFRAU CYMRU
BOOKS COUNCIL of WALES

LOTTERY FUNDED

Gathering

WOMEN OF COLOUR
ON NATURE

edited by
Durre Shahwar &
Nasia Sarwar-Skuse

Contents

Foreword

A cursory glance in any bookshop or library reveals that books on nature and climate crisis are predominantly written by white authors, while writers of colour are often overlooked. Yet the impact of the climate crisis is felt keenly by marginalised communities worldwide, particularly in the Global South. It is precisely this absence of intersectional stories, and the desire to amplify nature writing by women of colour, that led to the creation of this anthology.

Gathering arose out of a residency Durre undertook a few years ago, in which she explored her connection with the Welsh landscape as a woman of colour. She came to the end of that residency realising that there was more to be done; more writing and art by people of colour about nature, more inclusion of our voices in the fight to save our planet, and more autonomy over what we write about and how we write about it. Following insightful conversations between Durre and Nasia, the project gained its momentum.

Gathering felt fitting then as a title. A noun and a verb at once, signifying a move away from the individual into the collective, physically, and symbolically as this anthology does. The Welsh word for anthology is 'blodeugerdd'. When translated literally, 'blodeu' means 'flowers' and 'cerdd' usually means 'poem' or 'verse'. So 'the flowers of verse'. The essays in *Gathering* aren't poems or 'flowery' in the way that a literal meaning of both of those words might imply, nor in the way that writing by women about nature often gets negatively labelled as – quaint and twill. But what they do contain are different textures, colours, and scents that a verse of flowers might do. There are essays about the benefits of cold sea swimming, overcoming fear of solo hikes, the joy of discovery, the heartache of loss, the symbiosis of nature and faith, complex historical and contemporary narratives of exploitation and environmental destruction, as well as narratives of hope. All these essays underly a personal aspect that speaks to the embodied connection that we all have to whatever part of this earth that we occupy. The writers centre the environment from a backdrop to a protagonist, inviting us to explore the outer landscapes and the depths of our inner selves.

Gathering also evokes thoughts from Homi K. Bhabha's essay 'DissemiNation' in which he writes about the gathering of scattered people, converging, and sharing lived experiences to create a singular fact of historical importance. Similarly, this anthology is a gathering of women of colour's voices scattered across Britain, coming together to write on nature, creating a record of their diverse reflections, and experiences. It is a powerful act of writing themselves into conversations on nature.

It felt important to include this many different perspectives, voices, and styles of writing to reflect the way that nature is made up of so many layers that come together or pull apart. We didn't set out to achieve a conclusive, definitive, or an authoritative book on nature. We set out to provide an instigation, to evoke curiosity, and to explore. To be playful, celebratory and gentle at times, and at other times, angry, bold, and defiant. And rightly so.

Yet, despite these varying perspectives, there are a dozen or more essays that could have been included. We hope that *Gathering* is the beginning of a larger conversation; that people feel themselves reflected in these words, or feel inspired to write their own, and that more spaces are created for people of colour to express ourselves unapologetically and beautifully as the writers in this book have.

The writers showcased in *Gathering* open doors to understanding and shift paradigms. They dismantle barriers and challenge stereotypes, inspiring a more inclusive literary world where all voices can thrive and contribute to the collective narrative. They foster an environment of empathy and shared experience through their unique perspectives. Their words build bridges across cultures and communities, connecting readers from all walks of life. We hope that *Gathering* serves as a testament to the strength of personal storytelling in these challenging times, fosters meaningful connections and sparks profound conversations, so that we find ourselves renewed with hope for the future.

We invite readers to embark on this transformative journey with us, traverse the pages of this anthology, immerse in the visions painted by these writers, and feel the pulse of nature resonate within your heart. Let us gather to celebrate and remind ourselves that nature belongs to all, and that only through collective appreciation and understanding can we protect and nurture our precious planet.

- Durre Shahwar &
Nasia Sarwar-Skuse

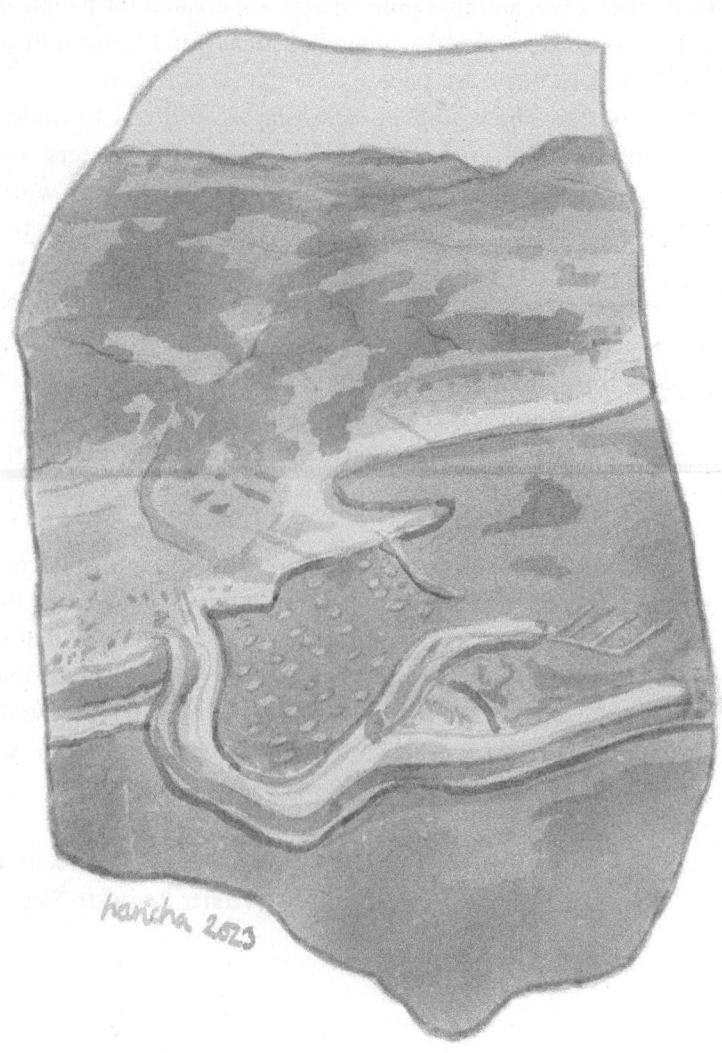

hanicha 2023

Image description: black and white illustration of an aeriel view of Lyme Regis showing hills in the distance and piers going into the sea with boats in the harbour.

A British-Ghanaian in the West Country

On symbols, myths and reimagining the British Countryside

LOUISA ADJOA PARKER

For too long, there has been a commonly held perception of the British countryside, which often evokes images of green fields and cattle with heads bent to the grass, or villages with windy roads and quaint, thatched cottages. Some might think of tea in the afternoon: scones and jam and thick yellow cream. Or the sea, with its dancing pinpricks of light, and long stretches of shingle or sand. Or farms, mud, tractors, smells of manure, glimpses of rare birds. It is a place many Brits like to holiday in, and there tends to be a somewhat romanticised view of rural Britain. Whatever springs to mind, the British countryside has long been presented as a space which is inhabited by – and exists purely for – people who are white. Tucked within this image is the idea that rurality represents the past, an imagined Golden Age, a simpler era, untouched by the trappings of modernity (which includes all the immigrants who came with it). And yet, although at first glance it might appear that the British countryside *is* predominantly inhabited by white people (at least in comparison with urban areas), its history is intertwined with Empire, colonialism, and slavery. In fact, as many of us are beginning to realise, the very symbols we take to represent Englishness – tea and sugar and country estates – are rooted in this history.

Alongside this, racism is often considered an urban issue – it doesn't exist in rural Britain because there aren't any people to be racist *to* there, right? At least, that's the pervading opinion that's long been present: 'there's no problem here.' Yet the idea that African, Asian, and other global majority heritage people are purely urban dwellers is a myth. Many global majority people who migrated to the UK settled in cities, yes, but not exclusively – we have multiple identities and we have inhabited multiple spaces, like anyone else. This idea that Black/Asian equals urban seeps into many areas of everyday life – from advertising to music to football to literature to TV and film. People within the Black British aesthetic, for instance, are often presented as one homogenous being, all trainers and/or nails, wearing the latest clothes, speaking in the same London-Caribbean hybrid slang ('urban' slash 'street'). Here, I want to share my lived experience of being a Black woman of British-Ghanaian heritage in rural Britain, as well as exploring symbols of rurality and how we can make space for global majority voices within them.

My Black African father came from Accra, Ghana in the 1960s and married my white English mother from Reading. I was born in Yorkshire in 1972, which was a time of open, hostile racism in the UK; to be of mixed heritage was tough. Just before my thirteenth birthday, after my parents split up, I moved from Cambridgeshire with my mum and siblings to Paignton. South Devon was familiar – I'd been going to visit my English grandparents there since I was six. But the reality of living in a seaside town was different to being a visitor there – you see the rot under the veneer, the darkness that hides underneath the sunlit towns where people go for sun, sea, and sand. You soon learn the land itself is infused with racism, along with other 'isms,' and that for those viewed as outsiders, life can be hard.

Our new home was opposite bluebell woods. The first thing I noticed about Devon was that it was entirely white. There were no other brown-skinned people around, or if there were, I didn't see any. The town I had left was surrounded by countryside, but it had been more multicultural. Here in Devon, other than my siblings, I was 'the only one.' And my difference did not go unnoticed by the local children. Most of the boys racially abused me and made it obvious they saw me as a female body to sexually experiment on, not as a 'proper girl' they'd be proud to be seen with. The girl next door was generally kind, although she merrily informed me that her dad hadn't wanted 'blacks' living next door. He was, nevertheless, friendly enough when he got to know us. As far as I am aware, these kids – and their parents – had never seen a Black or brown person before, other than on the telly.

The land around me soon became my home, a second skin I inhabited. I explored the woods, climbing the steep paths strewn with rotting leaves. I walked our dog and played with my so-called friends, chucking firelighters into piles of leaves, trying my first cigarette, having my first kiss. As I got older, I found solace in the woods, and at times I'd take myself off to sit on a tree branch, watching the world go by. A mile away was Preston beach, with its terracotta sand and cliffs, where you could walk over the damp sand to Paignton, with its rusty pier and games arcades. I wasn't a strong swimmer but enjoyed swimming in the shallow edges of the sea. In Totnes, where I went to school, there was the river Dart as well as woods and fields; spaces where I'd hang out with my friends, away from adult eyes. I took the land for granted the way young people tend to do – it was simply there. I didn't appreciate its full beauty until I was older.

And yet the reality of being a Black/mixed teenage girl in these spaces was a strange, challenging, and often upsetting one. Although I'd grown up with racism, here it was supersized, like stepping back in time. My face looked wrong against this rural backdrop, this place of sea and green and palm trees. People like me, I was told, belonged in cities, and yet, here I was! What was I doing here? Where was I *really* from? Like many young people of mixed heritage, I struggled with my identity. An added layer for me was that of rurality. I had no role models in the countryside. I didn't know what to wear, how to style my hair, I didn't know how to *be*. So, like most teenagers, I wore the clothes my friends were wearing, tried, unsuccessfully, to style my hair like a white person's. I wanted to be white and thin and have long straight hair. I hated being me. I escaped into a world where I was obsessed with boys (then men) who didn't love me, as well as smoking, drinking and drugs.

When I was nineteen, I moved with my baby daughter over the Devon border into Dorset, to a small seaside town of Lyme Regis, famous for its fossils and literary connections. I went on to have two more daughters as a solo parent and wanted to bring my children up in what seemed like a safe space: low crime, white sand and gold-topped cliffs, a silvery light like no other in the sky above the bay. It was the 1990s now, and no-one wanted to be a racist. Yet in some ways it was safe, and in others it wasn't. My daughters and I experienced daily microaggressions, comments about, and the touching of, our hair, racist jokes, and hearing inappropriate terminology and racism towards other ethnic groups. A friend once explained at length how she hated all the Asians coming to Britain.

'What about the Raj?' I said, 'What Britain did to India? The famines?'

'F**k me,' she replied, 'I don't know anything about that! I was too busy chasing boys at school to learn *anything*.'

I bumped into the same friend years later in the supermarket she worked in, after I'd moved away. She started on about Brexit and how we had 'too many immigrants.'

'Mate, I'm the *daughter* of an African immigrant,' I said, finally empowered by knowledge and the recent cultural shift in a collective understanding of race. 'I think we're going to have to agree to disagree on this one.'

My acceptance of myself and embracing my Black, rural identity has been a long journey. The turning point came when I was studying, and learned about Black British history, across the UK and in the countryside. I learned that we have been coming here for centuries, as – amongst other things – enslaved African 'servants', soldiers, sailors, entertainers, refugees, writers and abolitionists, and more recently, students, migrant workers, healthcare and catering workers. A fuller, reimagined history of rural spaces helps us all understand that we are connected, and that migration is not a contemporary phenomenon. It helped me to understand I have the right to belong. My journey also included working hard to undo the racism I'd internalised as a child, as well as researching and writing extensively about rural racism and diverse history in rural areas. Only now, in my fifty-first year, do I feel I fully belong in this space, and in my own skin. I am a Black woman of mixed heritage who lives in the countryside, and that's okay.

My research also led me to understand what it is like for others, that people with African, Asian, and other global majority heritage experience racism, which ranges from micro-aggressions to verbal and physical assaults. Although we are individuals, with different backgrounds and protective factors in place, there are many commonalities. Most of us witness and/or experience racism, to some degree. Many of us feel isolated without others who share our ethnic heritage. We are both highly *visible* – we stand out, and can't 'blend in' – and *invisible*, when it comes to being heard and represented.

There is so much power in representation. The first time I saw an image of a Black woman in the countryside was like finding a nugget of gold. The photo, in which the woman, in white jacket and boots, headwrap, camera in her lap, her head turned away from the camera, was part of a series called *Pastoral Interlude* by the photographer Ingrid Pollard. It was beautiful, and it subverted the idea of who belonged in the countryside, opening the doors for people like me.

Another pivotal moment was reading the poem 'In My Country' by Jackie Kay. I related so much to her poetics of walking in the countryside as a Black woman, I felt I had been seen – here was someone who *knew*, who got it.

There have been several changes in recent years when it comes to conversations around 'race' and ethnicity in rural spaces. There has been a shift in the demographics in the countryside over the past couple of decades. In the southwest where I live, there has been a visible increase in the numbers of global majority people living in and visiting the region. As well as this, since the murder of George Floyd and spread of the Black Lives Matter movement, there has been a shift in local organisations' understanding of racism and a clear desire to do more (or at the very least, to be *seen* to be doing more). There has also been increased interest in who is accessing the countryside with a focus on 'race' and class, and a shift in the ways we tell the histories of rural spaces; all part of a wider, global movement to decolonise our education systems, public spaces, as well as hearts and minds. Decolonisation can be a contentious issue, with some rejecting the need for it at all, and others disagreeing on the best way it should be done. I understand that for some, there is a real fear that our national identity and heritage may be lost, replaced with the unfamiliar, strange and 'woke.' Yet for me, it can only be a good thing – undoing the wrongs of the past, making space for diverse stories to be told, telling the stories of both colonisers and the colonised, and in doing so, shining a light on the long, dark shadow of Empire.

At the time of writing, I have been thinking about symbols of rurality, who they represent, and how these can be widened out to include ethnically diverse people. Recently, I went to meet with Professor Corrine Fowler, author of *Green Unpleasant Land*, to talk to her for her forthcoming book. As I drove through the village of Tolpuddle, where we were meeting to walk and talk, I reflected on how going to strange villages has never felt safe. I found myself scanning my surroundings as I drove, and noticed a Black binman, chatting and laughing with a white person. *It must be okay here*, I thought, irrationally. But as I drove past the St George's flags and houses, I started thinking more about the symbols of rural village life and who and what they represent.

'I've never seen a Black woman driving a tractor,' I said to Corrine, as we walked through the Dorset countryside. 'Or any woman, for that matter. It's usually young white men.' And there are spaces within villages that feel particularly unsafe. I won't, for example, walk into a country pub alone. That moment when the room goes silent, and people's heads swivel as one towards you feels too much to bear. *Where are you from?* they seem to say, *and what are you doing in our pub?*

Another symbol of country living which cuts across class: 'Hunting-shooting-fishing,' I said to Corrine as we watched men in waders cast their lines into the river. 'I'm a vegetarian! I don't do any of that sh*t.'

She laughed. 'I'd never heard them all put together like that.'

I talked to my husband about symbols when we went to the small seaside town of West Bay in Dorset recently. We looked around an antique centre, and I spotted a number of black figurines and masks which were parodies of Black people from the past. I braced myself, as I tend to do, for golliwogs, which are often to be found in shops and pubs in the countryside. For people like me, who grew up facing an ugly parody of myself grinning eerily from the marmalade jar over my breakfast, they are a symbol of hate and dehumanisation.

'But you can't get rid of the symbols,' my husband said. 'They're part of what makes the countryside.'

'I'm not saying we should get *rid* of them,' I replied, 'but open them up to include more people. Where are the images of Black families having a cream tea? Or doing outdoor activities? Where are the images of Black or Asian women with mud under their fingernails?'

'Like yours,' he said.

'Exactly!' I love gardening without gloves, digging my bare hands into the earth, in spite of the mud left under my fingernails afterwards. My nails, it has to be said, are definitely not 'on point.'

And the biggest, most prominent symbol of all: the country house and estate. Much work has uncovered links between these places and our colonial past, and we are learning what is hidden behind these walls, what might be buried in the grounds of manor houses. It is uncomfortable for some but imagine how uncomfortable it feels for people like me, who have known the history for some time. Here is a place I do see myself reflected, but most often, as a victim.

There are various campaigns, currently, to increase access to the countryside, to make space for a range of people, and for global majority people to reconnect with nature and the land. And yet there is still much to be done – simply having larger numbers of African and Asian diaspora people in the countryside is not enough. We need, as a community, to change the infrastructure, ensure everyone's needs are met, fully understand the history, ensure global majority people can see ourselves reflected in the landscape, and challenge racism and other forms of discrimination in all their guises.

In the countryside, already complex issues of identity and 'race' have further layers of complexity. Many from the wider white rural community often have little face-to-face interaction with people from ethnic backgrounds different to their own. But we live in the twenty-first century. The internet exists and there's a wealth of information out there. It's easier than ever before to learn about colonial legacies and 'race' and the experiences of those who have been marginalised and 'Othered.' It is possible and easy to learn beyond your own experience.

We need to dismantle myths and stereotypes and find ways to represent the full breadth of human beings in ways that are authentic. As well as this, people from the wider, white British community can act as allies to those of us who have been racialised as 'Other'. The beautiful rolling hills and coastlines are for all of us. Together, we can reimagine the British countryside (and all it represents) and make space so that everyone is welcomed.

Image description: black and white illustration of a square plot of land, divided into nine sections, each with various foliage growing from them.

Nature is Queer

We Could Learn a Thing or Two from That

JASMINE ISA QURESHI

I am a biologist. Well, I'm a failed biologist. I didn't enjoy academia and the symmetrical balance we as students were forced to teeter upon to reach an ending that I saw as just being the beginning again, but with a different flavoured topping.

Biology to me is magic. It is Sorcery. Squishy, living, breathing, toxic, untameable, nonsensical, dribbling, all-powerful magic. By magic, I am suggesting the abstract concept and title of 'magic' as pertaining to beauty, and 'chaotic' behavioural observation (chaos theory), chemistry – a science often referred to as 'magical' due to its explanation of natural processes in terms we cannot directly sense, and spontaneous reaction. I am suggesting that biology is an art of exploration. The art of asking questions, and the art of finding out.

Words such as 'magic', and 'art' are normally personifications of more emotionally charged subjects, such as literature, and music. However, these terms can and should be used for science-based subjects too, especially biology and ecology, thus closing the gap between 'creative' subjects, and seemingly 'non-creative, fact-based' subjects.

This gap ignores the intersectional and interwoven discrepancies that exist in all subjects and concepts. It limits the flexibility of perspectives that are needed to progress our understanding. Unlearning the bias of 'emotionless', and linear/binary science theory and study, helps us to collate the natural world into magic and art, and promotes a more 'passion-based' approach (which also seeks to topple false hierarchies, the viewing of nature as a simple 'resource', and promotes respect of the natural world, and by extension, the rest of the world).

Furthermore, this flexible, more creative approach, also allows gatekeeping to be disintegrated, and elitist methods of teaching and accessing resources around these subjects to be disallowed. Nomenclature – and its usage as a key factor of identification – may be a small part of what we see, and perhaps rudimental, but its influence cannot be ignored. It often acts as an obstacle to those without the specific experience or background to access its pre-empted concepts.

To me, biology, and indeed the behaviour of the natural world is the music produced by the alchemy of existence. Music must be studied with care and attention. The overall passion, flexible mindset, creative flair and love a musician has will be the deciding factor in the quality of music. The same is true for a biologist. For example, as an ecologist and someone with a specific love for entomology and invertebrates, if I am to study an animal in this environment, I must approach this study from an angle with as little anthropocentric bias as possible, because viewing wildlife with 'human characteristics' can cause entire conclusions to be drawn upon false pretences.

The patriarchal leadership in many of our societies does not exist in most insect colonies, suggesting a renewed understanding of how societies are formed or led in animal kingdoms. The care and attention I direct to my study will determine how much awareness I have of my subjects being worthy of respect as living organisms. Furthermore, the creative flair I allow in this study will progress it, as I find new ways of testing concepts and hypotheses that are as untethered to human behaviour as possible, all the while working against the common boundary of scientific review.

This approach is true of any scientist. But for a biologist, naturalist (professional or amateur), or anyone living in this world of chaotic, kinetic energy-powered soup, it is especially necessary. This approach promotes attention to detail, care, and respect of not just the study subject, but of your own emotions and identity.

So, if biology is part of this kinetic energy-powered soup, then I'm a soup witch. To be technical, a marine biologist. The bud of which grew from the branch of storytelling.

I wanted to be a storyteller first anyway; I remember scribbling away when I was younger and making films about the animals I saw. I wrote short stories and drew little comics about power-hungry scientists. I developed an intense interest in how things worked; how did bees know which flowers to travel towards. How did whales 'speak'. Why did planets revolve around the suns. Why does ice melt? Everything I do has grown from there.

My need to know how the world works led me to science, and my love of nature led me even more specifically to natural science and ecology. My storytelling habits now bore fruit where before they had been hidden away by our education system's Victorian-era roots. A system which was developed to enact 'crowd control' over large groups of working-class children, whilst their parents worked, often to prepare them for the same or similar line of work, usually under the control of private, home-educated superiors.

It channels children into singular lines of economically efficient work, and my breaking out of it propped me up along the way and drove me to reach out to jobs in journalism and science communication. It actually stopped me from leaving STEM (science, technology, engineering, and mathematics) many times, usually when I became disheartened with the work environment, convincing me that I could make this industry comfortable and euphoric for myself one day.

I am one of those writer-scientist-poet people. The ones who trip and stumble through careers (since I left university and during my studies I've had at least ten different jobs) as they hold on to the promise of exploring and telling everyone how awesome those adventures are.

I made my way up the mountain of Latin nomenclature and birds renamed after problematic leaders of boat trips; we often see the names of wildlife as their only name, however, studies usually discover a 'renaming' has occurred. Indigenous communities have previously allocated names, and these animals are then 'discovered' by colonialist collectors, and renamed after their expedition leaders. For example, a study found that the majority of eponymous bird names – birds named after a person – of up to 149 species in North America have been allocated names assigned by European and American naturalists in the nineteenth century. Of these, multiple are from figures associated with slavery and white supremacy, such as the McCown's longspur, a grassland bird that was named after Confederate general John Porter McCown, renamed after the protests around racist nomenclature forced the hands of ornithological organisations.

This resulted in a chase that has continued for all of my life. One for the magic and mayhem of biology.

The first taste of this magic was delicious. Addicting. Alluring and gourmet. It was a buzzing euphoric flavour of bumblebees and butterflies, woodlice and spiders.

The fascination with insects, invertebrates and entomology drew me in, and not strictly because I was a budding creepy crawly lover from the start, but almost out of a desperate thirst for natural life in the grey scape, I grew up in. A concrete tea caddy. Communities of spicy food, Urdu and Arabic.

Graffiti splattered walls, glass breaking at night, orange gauze and sparkling jewellery of aunties and cousins. Smog, Quranic readings, prayer, loud engines and nightlife that never slept cloaked me like an oversized tee. But I was in a bubble within a bubble.

The home-schooling of my early years, curated by my mother for me and my siblings, caught me before I fell into the sharp reality around me; I usually watched David Attenborough documentaries and *Springwatch*. These programmes weaved a complicated world. From whitened, elderly, soft music-filled chambers of fields – the people in them much the same as each other, never once darker than the clouds they stood under – to the exciting, gyrating, explosive monsters of the Amazon.

There was no in-between. The reason I stayed with my nose stuck in the soil and my face to the wind even when I felt pushed out or underrepresented in these areas as a voice, was because I felt my connection to be more than just interest. I felt connected to the very foundations of nature, I felt my exploration of the natural world was a reflection of the ecosystem that was my identity.

I needed to touch, explore, observe and hunt dragons that were smaller than my palm, but no less gorgeous and inspiring. That was my way to nature. To biology. To ecology.

At breakfast, I read Wikipedia pages and encyclopaedias of lands and creatures far, far away. I watched documentaries of a glossy, blue and green turquoise planet hanging in space. And spent time with my bugs of course.

This taste carried me to where I am today. But where I am today is a very different place to the start of my adventure. By this, I mean my arrival at queer ecology.

Queer ecology is not a term I coined from my thought library. It has been around since the 1970s, weaving its gossamer webs in between the shards of ecofeminism and gender theory. In its current and most developed form, it speaks to me so directly and intimately that it is a wonder that I did not see it as the subject to counter all subjects before it.

Simply put, queer ecology refers to the understanding and observation of ecology and biology in a manner that presents the natural world and all that it influences as an ever-changing, flexible spectrum. This defies the heteronormative binary bias, and anthropocentrism that is present as the key factor of biology and ecological learning today. It suggests that the behaviour that we have stapled to animals big and small, and used to cut them into the binaries of male and female, nature and society, and binaries beyond this, are a result of assumptions. The assumptions that they are reflective of the behaviour we exhibit are, resultant of our societal evolution.

An evolution that is a result of patriarchal development, made to thrive by the rise of colonialism and conservative religious practices. We, therefore, emphasise this binary, as it is forced upon us from birth, and use it to determine and develop a lifestyle. This is often of various stereotypes and norms, which influence our understanding of the world. Thus, continuing the vicious cycle as we unknowingly reinforce it upon others in our circles.

The various manifestations of this binary-based autonomy control include expression – clothing, behaviour, and desires. – conservative societies with Eurocentric values reinforce this bias. For example, femininity is associated with dresses, tighter clothing, or having a higher diversity of clothing options. There is strong evidence to suggest certain mannerisms and feelings have been structured as per binary gender expression (vulnerability, early emotional maturity, and others, are seen as 'feminine' in nature, and the 'opposite' of these, or the lack of, is therefore 'masculine').

Thus, a person wishing to validate their identity and expression becomes limited by these structures.

Of course, this is a very generalised perspective, and it does differ as per the environment one grows up in, and the influences, such as cultural norms, differences of opinion, and circles of friendship, family and acquaintances, But what is true is that this is the average of behaviour, and so most of the population is affected by the binary bias in this way, and importantly, our perspective of the natural world is structured as such too.

The rise of queer theory sought to break this cycle and bring about an awareness of our spectrum-based existence, and the interactions that make up ourselves and the ecosystems we are present within. This ideology was to be the antithesis to the approach that, 'humanity is a unique and separate being from other animals and nature', and thus disregards us so strongly as a blueprint for the behaviour and existence of all other life on Earth.

With this fresh understanding and the awareness that life itself is not as cut and dry as we previously understood it to be, come new answers to climate change; more direct and community-led responses to wildlife decline, and a more progressive and overall clearer vision of the inner workings of ecology and conservation. For example, a climate crisis policy that centres on globalisation would be bolstered by a queer outlook. It would promote intersectional thinking and invite a wider range of perspectives to the table.

The understanding of queer ecology, and implementation of its values, would also be incredibly useful to environmental policy, which at present is very much tethered to the main influencers of societal structure (in this case, the global north). By disconnecting this political vision from corporate power and economic output, and prioritising lived experiences and guidance, the focus shifts to amplifying marginalised voices and benefits everyone through a grassroots approach rather than the current 'top down' structure.

Queer ecology quite rightly leans heavily on the definition of a spat-out word of jumbled obscenity; queer. The word meaning, 'different', urges all who speak it and live by it to approach all items in their grasp from a 'non-conformity' and non-stereotypical perspective. Typically the most non-conformate and most 'queer' thinkers are those whose lived experience defies the 'average' presentation of a member of society: Eurocentric, cisgender, cisnormative, white, heteronormative, straight, male and female, middle/upper class, able-bodied, neurotypical adult human beings.

Anyone defiant of these norms presents an ideal breeding ground for queer thought and a queer understanding of ecology and nature. This comes with the challenges of a society that caters first and foremost to that 'average human being' standard. Thus, less time and resources are lent to queer thinkers to develop their alternative methods of thought and understanding, in an already hostile environment to non-conformity. The queer thinkers are now far and few, resultant of a reality that takes from your will to thrive and pumps energy into the need to survive.

I am one of those queer thinkers. My upbringing was in deep-rooted traditional and cultural surroundings. The strict Sunni Islamic teachings, coupled with Pakistani food, language, and community, gave me pride but at the same time limited my stride. Through the struggle of escaping an environment I loved (and would come to miss), and further strengthening my queer thought journey by understanding my transness, and indeed the non-binary status of my identity, I came to see nature as so much closer to myself. I saw that the non-binary in me cried out for no labels in terms of my expression and for respect for my heteronormative trauma and growth.

Further reading into the workings of genetic and hormone development, generally in anthropology, allowed me to see how we first develop as a non-binary system. It is then the patriarchal defined, 'reproductive binary', that assigns a 'role' to us. This is usually based on an arcane understanding of the human purpose (producing children and passing on genetic information) and of our place in society based on the fleshy growths between our legs. Both we have come to use as identifiers of gender, and thus roles and status in society. I began to read the pieces I never knew existed. Articles on differing levels of hormones in humans and animals. The differing number of sexes existing in species. The differences between gender, sex, identity and behaviour. Intersex wildlife and people, how racism has heavily influenced gender expression. How it has led us to come to conclusions on nature, and how patriarchal norms and scientists have incorporated these problematic and limiting assessments into the very systems teaching us and our children about biology.

I started to question everything I knew, and everything I had been brought up to believe, and with that questioning came the ultimate question. Why was I advocating for wildlife. Why did I care so much about the environment. Why did I want to understand myself?

The answer was a heady mix of a passion for my subject, a duty to a cause bigger than me, a responsibility to others less privileged than me, and a need to thrive instead of simply surviving.

Fascinatingly, the main reason many people love and protect wildlife is because of another, less coveted or advertised part of nature, us. We often forget, through the mainstream version of ecology and 'activism', that human beings, are a part of the global ecosystem, and thus a very intrinsic part of nature. We are not so displaced from the crisis of the environment and its workings as we are taught to believe.

I am passionate about nature because it excites me, and it excites me because of its diversity and beauty. This appreciation for these key aspects becomes greater the more reflective I am of my musicality. The responsibility to conserve wildlife leads to an awareness of the communities and societies that lean upon it, and are interwoven within it, and indeed have lived this way for centuries. The awareness of the fact that the most marginalised groups of people in the world are affected the worst by habitat loss, climate change and wildlife decline, and are simultaneously the people least responsible for these various crises, can only come through a reflection of our privilege. A sure result of the reflection that comes via the usage of queer ecology as a format of study.

Whoever we are, we possess certain degrees of privilege in multiple areas and aspects of our lives. It is through the systematic and detailed reflection of our backgrounds, environments, and learning, and understanding of these areas, that it becomes possible to address the problems deeply programmed in our society and behaviour. It is then easier to identify the most marginalised and underprivileged; who beforehand would have existed under our radar. These people are suffering, and the privileged pay little heed until the crises and issues of both the planet and society affect them directly.

Queer thought drives the progress of diverse and accessible action, community-based learning, and thriving alongside one another. It builds a healthy respect for the natural world and its wonders, which includes the peoples and societies that exist alongside, and because of it.

If ecology is the art of finding out about things, then queerness is the art of difference and questioning the status quo. Queer thought, therefore, allows you to understand concepts with greater flexibility.

Whilst queer ecology helps us to understand nature, nature helps us understand our own queerness. There are multiple examples in wildlife where stereotypical gender identifiers, (hair, genitalia, body fat, size, reproductive capabilities), is shown to be a simple case of differing hormone levels, and a result often-times of environmental pressures (offspring mortality rates, geographical location, natural selection, genetic diversity). This defies the 'facts' of gender and identity that have been forced upon us as humans.

My learning of my love for myself, and the trans, defiant, non-conforming body that I have, along with the ways I choose to express myself, have been achieved only through my passionate love of nature's flexibility. This I have combined with an understanding of its changing attitude to the ways that every organism that exists in natural ecosystems expresses itself, both phenotypically and genotypically.

The deeply complex natural world is astoundingly understanding of our shallow approaches to its mechanisms. From it, we can learn acceptance, respect and the importance of diverse perspectives. Whilst it also teaches humility and contentment in our place, we should understand that we are a special kind of magic. Independent existence and thought give us the quality of invention and reinvention. Not a magic *only* assigned to us, but one that we use fantastically.

This shift in perspective and understanding doesn't have to strictly adhere to Mother Nature's rule book, but it also shouldn't solely reflect our terms. Nature is undeniably queer.

We all have some introspection to do to truly understand ourselves to such an extent, but by dissecting and analysing ourselves – perhaps with a touch of that precious magic – we will discover just how much we have in common with nature.

haricha 2023

Image description: black and white illustration of The Stones of Scotland in Regent Road Park, Edinburgh, with stones arranged in a circle with a pine tree in the centre, swaying in the wind.

The Stones of Scotland / (a)version

ALYCIA PIRMOHAMED

S eeds and their scattering are irrefutably linked with metaphors of (dis)placement: of errantry, of wandering, of migration. Agents of pollination are part of this cycle: the orchid, the moth, the wind. These are nice images. It's evocative to transpose nature onto an ever-searching consciousness, to elect a symbol for the self that eventually finds soil. This is a compelling mythology.

.

I'm constantly entangled in a complicated intimacy with my Muslim upbringing. I wake up some mornings, and prayer finds me as naturally as language. This ritual tugs me forward into the whole of my day with its vast energy. Just last night I dreamt that my younger sister and I were together preparing for evening prayer – though we are, in actuality, over 6,000 kilometres apart, and with a deep mysterious ocean between us.

This dream is strange; it makes me curious. Of all of us in my immediate family, my younger sister and I have strayed the furthest from our faith. But a dream like this one reminds me that, *yes*, I carry a strong remnant of spirituality within me. I catch myself praying all the time. Even, it appears, within the metaphysical boundaries of my dreams. In a back and forth, teetering, blurry series of movements, I participate in a push and pull: I practice my faith and then I let it go. I pray to Allah and then I displace Them to the back of my mind. I am aligned and then I am not.

·

When I think I need its comfort and belief the most, my faith eludes me –

In spring 2020, two things coalesced. This season marked the first lockdown in Scotland, reeling as it still is from the Covid-19 pandemic. The lockdown also knotted with the whole of Ramadan. In self-isolation, afraid and lonely, I found it difficult to feel connected to anything, but I found it especially difficult to feel connected to Islam. I was displaced from my family who remained the strongest link I had to my faith. During this season, the distance between Edmonton and Edinburgh seemed greater than ever, perhaps too great a distance for even my dreams to travel.

Ramadan that year took on a different, unrecognisable shape, one edged with trepidation. In response, I resolutely listened to prayers through my old phone speakers, though they were ribbed with static. I tried to appreciate in (digital) moments with my family more completely. My mother and father and aunts and uncles all separately sent me images of spring flowers annotated with blessings in lieu of videos of family gatherings.

And though I wouldn't realise it until much later, I was *collecting*. By that, I mean I was beginning to squirrel away the anxiety of the pandemic in my body, which has unfurled now into its own new, marked, and unequivocal margins. I didn't know it then, but three years into the future, I would be weighed down by it. Eventually, my body would transform into the kind of emotional and physical shape that could just barely contain the disquiet.

Around that time, as the cracked screen of my phone became a kind of habitat, not quite a home, but a place I lived in, someone I trust advised me to find a way to *dislodge what is lodged* – swim in a river, perhaps, she said. I thought a lot about those words, how they made me notice something invasive and unbelonging in my body. Within a few months, I was also forced to turn to the question of how to tend to the act of *lodging*. The process. The way by which trauma leaks into a system and calcifies.

That spring, in my pursuit to feel close to Islam despite these chasms, I vowed to be more self-reflective; meditative; generous with myself and with others. I wanted to connect more deeply with my surroundings, with my community – and ultimately, as became evident over those asymmetrical months, with the natural world.

Eventually, to feel that connection I longed for, and perhaps in an effort to dislodge, I began an intentional practice of reading a poem by a South Asian woman outdoors every day. The poems would reify against the contours of spring – they were my river. This practice became a ritual, a form of spirituality in itself. I did this every day of Ramadan, looking ahead toward Eid. Through this act, walking and prayer intertwined.

•

One morning that spring, I had set out with the intention of walking to the crags, Edinburgh's city cliffside. I had decided early on that one of my treks that month would be toward this landmark; I was drawn to its unavoidable proof of this city's green verticality. The poem I was to read that day came from the pamphlet *bulbul calling* by Indo-Swiss poet and critic Pratyusha. This collection's shimmering voice is interspersed with inked line drawings that burgeon like a lifeline on the handmade cover.

My walk was cut short by weather. I found myself scattered amongst the familiar landscape near Easter Road. There, I was jostled by the wind and unable to journey where I had wanted to go. I didn't tread down the steps that would take me to the field behind Holyrood Palace, where a path would eventually curve toward the point that I'd begin my climb. Instead, moving against a rough ecological friction, I turned abruptly and made my way to Regent Road, succumbing to the vectors of strong winds that gasped around me.

The wind speed that day was 31 miles per hour. According to the Beaufort wind scale, I could call this wind a *moderate gale*. The moderate gale ushered me away from what I knew and toward the unexpected, as if I was a seed being carried along to some resting place where I'd eventually root, and bloom, and flourish.

'Wind was the invisible force powering colonial expansion,' writes poet and interdisciplinary artist J.R. Carpenter. The Beaufort Scale informs the structure of her modal piece, *This Is a Picture of Wind,* where poetry was 'randomly generated in part by live wind data and in part by the inexorable passage of time.'

The wind, I have come to realise, is a cartographer – a mixture of biology, art, and technology. It is a system that both surveys the past and tells the future.

•

I'm both uncertain and reassured when it comes to definitions of diaspora. I find the image of the wayward seed compelling, but I'm also distraught by it. I crave rootedness because rootedness is shaped so much like belonging. But then I'm jolted by the sharp reminder of what I ache to root into.

Even the word *belonging* seems to me, now, like a kind of marker. A tell. An emotional landscape that the white gaze has redesigned into a slogan.

Besides, how can I root in any place where modernity and Westernisation, heteropatriarchy, and capitalism are primary markers of belonging? Where my body must flourish only in accordance to the coloniser's system of oppression? Where the English language elides my first tongues.

I think of Priyamvada Gopal's *Insurgent Empire*, which interrogates 'the tenacious assumption that the most significant conceptions of "freedom" are fundamentally "Western" in provenance.'

Or of the mathematical asymptote: the long line that can get close, so close, to touching its nearby curve. Line and curve are in proximity, the difference between them almost becoming zero. But they do not touch, and they never will. The asymptote is the limit. I am the limit by which the oppressor can know themselves.

All of this because once my ancestors were forced by the wind and arrived elsewhere.

·

My earliest memory of prayer is also an early memory of learning how to read. I'm six years old and in my parents' bedroom. We moved from this townhouse when I was eight, but somehow, more than other places I've lived, this particular home and its small blueprint is stark and defined in my memory. It's the first home I can remember; a unit at the end of a line of adjoined buildings, four families sharing walls against the backdrop of flat Albertan prairies.

I imagine walking down the narrow hallway, past the bathroom on my right, and arriving at the nightstand at my father's side of the bed. This is where he keeps his copy of his Quran, with its dark green cover. Beautifully bound, it is a bilingual edition with Arabic in the first half. I scan the script, black ink swooping across its pages in cursive peaks and percussions. It dips and travels and swells like the unending note of a long breeze. I've memorised a few words – but not enough to decode the language that I will never learn. Something in me flickers. I want to know what these pages hold. I think they will help me better understand my father. I switch to the English side.

The Quran is only meant to be recited in Arabic. Its revelations are truest in Arabic. I gaze at the two slippery hearts: Arabic and its English translations.

In primary school, I had been focused on learning how to read. How to shape English letters into their precise markings, tall, tree-like letters next to small eddies. There is an emphasis on *this* language, and this language is a storm. With its ongoing rains, English overruns the few hours every Saturday morning that I spend practicing my Duas.

On those Saturdays, I lag behind in my recitation. But, with an uneasy pride, I find I can quickly memorise a verse in English. My prayer slips away from me, imperceptibly.

•

As an immigrant and settler in Canada, I, too, am marked by Westernised modernity. I am part of an ongoing colonial precedent. My archive is filled with the stories my father tells me about Dar es Salaam, where he grew up, my mother's inherited family recipes, the God I pray to, the ancestral remembrance of other ways of being. It is also the lived experience of being educated in the West, of working in the West, of submitting to academic models of the West – where the concept of decolonising the institution is problematised by the institution's very existence on stolen land.

In ongoing acts of displacement to places where Western consciousness and whiteness hold power, what are the social, historical, and political contexts that underscore future lived experiences?

Drifting, scattering, planting, rooting, blossoming, drinking in the Scottish rains, being pulled by its wind – yes, I embody all of this. All of this is simultaneously rupturing. I double and triple and multiply into an octet, continuously, until I am relational to everything all at once, river and stone. Until I am the asymptote journeying forever toward infinity.

I wake up one morning that spring and feel compelled to recite tasbih: Subhan Allah, thirty-three times. My body relaxes and my anxiety quietens. If invasive experiences and feelings have lodged into my body, at least there is also this. The way the body might remember something ancestral, the way memories thread from generation to generation, the way love slips in, unnoticed.

But stories too, our childhood memories and our inheritances, have their own wind; they are their own gales. We are so full of stories. Perhaps it is in art where we can plant and uproot all of them at once.

•

In the UK, as pandemic restrictions ease, I find myself reading my work aloud to predominantly white audiences. Under harsh lighting with my body pointed toward a room of unfamiliar faces, I recite my poetry about the solitary heron at Lochend Park, about elk and their muscular strength in Jasper, about Florence, Oregon where oysters gather on oceanic ridges of the Pacific. And doubly, these poems are tinged with the complexity of my faith. I river between sexual desire, queerness, and womanhood, touching on the way these aspects weave together with my Muslim faith. The elk, their antlers poised against green vine, are symbolic of a lesson: *it is as if Allah himself has approached me* to depart Their divine knowledge. Through my poetry, through its sinews of imagery and introspection, I attempt to accept the alternating calcifications and softnesses of my body. I try to find a way to accept my body as it exists beside my religion.

Poet and academic Kazim Ali writes, 'the body is not the opposite of the spirt, nor are physical matters oppositional to abstract ideas of the spirit.'

I allow myself to feel at peace when I pray and when I don't. I allow myself to feel distraught when prayer eludes me. I allow my body to be my body, whether engaged in the religious experience of counting or gathered in the arms of an intimate partner. I remind myself that belief is also a plot of land on which we can grow the seeds of what we love.

•

When I read my poetry to one of those predominantly white audiences three years later, I speak briefly about my practice during Ramadan in 2020. A part of me, I admit, wants to prove to them that my writing about faith *is* also nature writing. I want to undercut insidious thought processes that categorise me as: either a Muslim writer or a nature writer, but never both. Whiteness churns through my context like a machine.

Historically, white poets in the mainstream, in the canon, have also been writing from their sociopolitical contexts, elevating their content with their lived experiences. It is their constructed familiarity that disguises such content as universal, that hides the mechanism of categorisation. But, subjective experience and positionality, whatever a person's sociopolitical context may be, will leave its traces on a poem.

After the reading, a woman comes up with a bemused look on her face. She says to me, something like 'Ramadan in Edinburgh? ... how fascinating.' As if it is remarkable that these two realms, these two 'categories,' could ever coexist. And it is painful to see how in so few words, an entire community of Muslims in Edinburgh with a long history is erased.

There is no reply that can reassemble an archive that so strongly displaces bodies like mine from the centre.

•

At Regent Road Park, there is a monument where 32 stones are arranged in a circle, and in the centre of that circle is a pine tree. That spring morning, I stood within the orbital boundary and looked straight ahead. From there, I had a clear view of the glaciated remains that marked the crags, the crags which had been my original destination.

The stones had travelled from Aberdeen, Stirling, East Ayrshire... and now, they are displaced together here, in Edinburgh. Grey granite, red sandstone, andesite, all of it side by side.

In *Cultivation and Catastrophe: The Lyric Ecology of Modern Black Literature*, the scholar Sonya Posmentier writes that 'Hybridity and diaspora are etymologically related to organic life, signalling the need to consider these cultural concepts ... as living metaphors.'

What is the distance between arriving and becoming? When is a landscape no longer a landscape, but an organ in my body? When does my body begin to entwine with a landscape, acknowledging its part in an immense and spindly, endlessly reaching network?

When does a collection of stones begin to house the moss of a different place?

•

Around the time of my walk, I came across an online archive of the *Harriet Books* blog on the Poetry Foundation website. As a past contributor, Bhanu Kapil wrote a sequence on divination. In one of her posts from 2012, she specifically brings together poetry and tarot. Pulling a card for poetry, Kapil reveals The Five of Stones. In her article, this card is also referred to as The Ghosts of Healing.

Reading that article at that time felt serendipitous, as if – though she had written it almost a decade before – Kapil had pulled the card just for me, and specifically for this wayward and errant walk.

The Stones of Scotland, arranged in a circle, stone next to stone, are embedded in Regent Road Park. Lichen and moss hold them in place. They are part of a geological and geometrical organisation. I am aware of their past lives, but will only ever know them here, where their context is changed by the crags behind them, the tree between them, the city around them. By my very presence that day, accidental as it was.

As the blog post ends, Kapil cites Rachel Pollack's interpretation of this card, and I am drawn to how it holds spirituality, history, imagination alongside the literal:

Here in the Five of Stones we see an image of deep spiritual healing. The ghostlike images (based on rock paintings) seem to rise out of the stone, or to come forward. Readings for spiritual wisdom can produce such deep healing, connecting soul to spirit. They ground us in a sacred reality that is both as genuine as stones and mysterious as ghosts. Through wisdom readings we confront spiritual ideas directly and can begin to see that such things may after all be real.

It is an apt card for poetry, and in a way, it is an eerily too perfect encounter that day during Ramadan, when I seek the solace of the divine while engaged with The Stones of Scotland. In the stone garden, I feel momentarily reflected: *seen*: metaphorically, metaphysically, and literally. I make a spiritual space for new stones, the stones I carry, always: the mossy rock from Alberta, the wet, mooring agate on the Oregon coast, the red clay from Mtwara. I think of how even in my imagination, they have changed over the years, echoing with new movements. It would be three years, for example, before I would see Alberta's shield of rocks again. And so, they would become more and more blurred and unreal in memory.

Here, adrift next to the Scots Pine, I read Pratyusha's poem, '(a)version,' which feels – again – coincidental. After all, this reading is a version of what I set out to accomplish, a different version than I expected. Its own peculiar kind of aversion.

Her words echo on the periphery of this multidirectional journey. In her lines, riveting and rife with the Ganga River, there is the suggestion of what we carry, or even *how* we carry across multiplicity –

'My grandmother gives me a shell, because I should keep the water with me.'

•

'Migration stories are skin memories,' Sara Ahmed writes, 'Memories of different sensations that are felt on the skin.'

And I suppose, then, they must also be wind memories. There is that sensation, that deep push and pull, that grazes my face, my neck, my arms, *my skin*. And created at the meeting of contradiction – high and low pressure – there is something in between about it too. As if wind itself is the hinge that swings in every and all directions.

Works Cited

Ali, Kazim. 'A Conversation with Kazim Ali'. *Stay Thirsty Magazine,* 2017. staythirstymagazine.blogspot.com/p/kazim-ali. html

Carpenter, JR. 'Mapping Place | Troubling Space.' *the digital review,* no. 00, 2020. doi.org/10.7273/hrcm-r304

Carpenter, JR. *this is a picture of wind.* Penned in the Margins, 2020.

Gopal, Priyamvada. *Insurgent Empire.* Verso Books, 2019.

Kapil, Bhanu. 'Divination 3: (For Poetry): Frida Kahlo and The Ghosts of Healing.' Harriet Books Blog, Poetry Foundation, 2012. poetryfoundation.org/harriet-books/2012/04/divination-3-for-poetry-frida-kahlo-and-the-ghosts-of-healing

Posmentier, Sonya. *Cultivation and Catastrophe.* John Hopkins University Press, 2017.

Pratyusha. *Bulbul calling.* Bitter Melon 苦瓜, 2020.

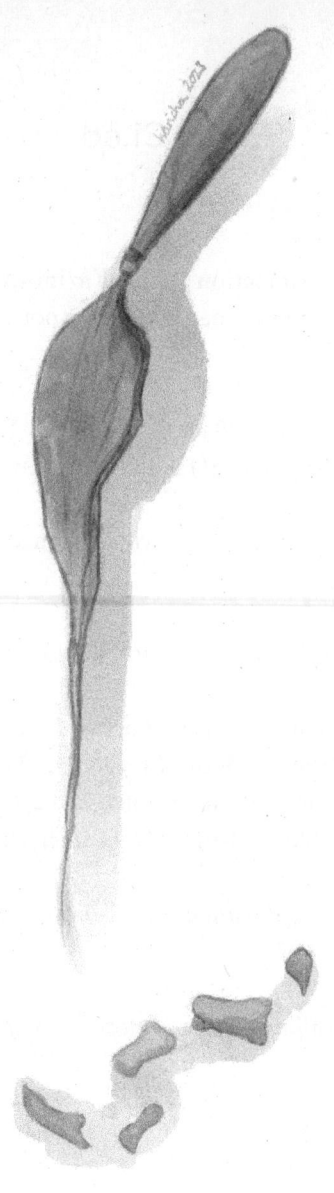

Image description: black and white abstract illustration of a trowel melting, with five bones resting below it.

A Pencil, a Trowel and a Dinosaur Bone

KATHERINE CLEAVER

I had a life before writing. I walked a different path that led me down many rabbit holes and roads, in both education and work, all revealing different landscapes, before I found the path that I currently walk. I was living in a right-wing heartland and starting out on a career I wasn't sure I wanted. I had been to a university that allowed me to disappear into the shadows; I was seen and yet no one saw me. No one pushed to see what made me tick. I had lecturers who would throw dinosaur bones at me and ask me to reconstruct them, but no one wanted to work with me. I was the Other.

The degree was a mix of art and science; show biology through the image. I was obsessed with creating artwork from an iron rich spring that fell out of a brilliantly green hill to bleed red into the watercourse. The lecturer took me by the hand and we stood, watching until rain started to fall, forcing us back toward the car. I loved the colour with the bacteria and algae strings, the hillside had become something strangely horrific, its guts spilling out. Yet this was a normal process, something that happens in the area, iron escaping and dissolving. I would have stood in the rain, transfixed until the light had faded.

The lecturer saw my focus and sent me to a man who had, in a shed at the bottom of his garden, a dozen microscopes all with a camera on top. 'I know the seep,' the man said, leaning a little too close. He pulled out several slides, each one filled with the brightest of colours. So beautiful and yet alien. Deeply red shapes that looked organic next to mustard yellow spines of geometric shapes. 'Use these,' he said. I went away thinking of my bleeding hill and how I could marry the science and the art. How it would work.

The course doesn't exist now – dissolved and disappeared – but at the time it was a brave new world, and we were looking at creating biological images. A place where you could marry the biology and art to create the unexpected. Creativity in the landscape; from dinosaurs to microbes and DNA. I loved it. Yet there was a problem: with one foot in the arts and another in the science, there was really no home. It was known that the scientists looked down on the artists and the artists scoffed at the scientists. Those of us on the joint course were in the middle, trapped. I remember that I needed to hinge my dissertation on science – there had to be something I could measure – so I decided the easiest thing to do was to look at the bugs and algae growing in the water. I figured a few days in the lab would give me enough information to write about the biodiversity in the blood red water. I talked to my supervisor, and he said, 'sounds good.' Then he told me I had to clear the lab time. I figured I just needed space and a microscope.

Now, in this university, the two departments of art and science were five miles apart, so it was a bit of a trek to find the Doc to clear lab time. If I had known about anything to do with research and universities, I should have realised that it was my supervisor's job to talk to this guy. He was the one who had cleared the project and the one with the most contacts. I was a student, struggling, not academically, but socially. My autism was worse; I couldn't meet eyes and every conversation was a fight against anxiety. By the time I reached the Doc's door it was closed, and I was tired and sweaty. All I wanted was a quick word, a note that I could have a go with the microscopes, and I would take it from there. The dissertation was already planned, and I was looking forward to it. That is what pushed me to raise my hand and knock.

'Yes?' the voice was not a happy one, but I shrugged. This man had marked one piece of my work and given me a high 80. He may not remember me, but I was certain I could stand shoulder to shoulder with any of the science undergraduates.

I opened the door and saw his desk was a good ten feet away for me to walk forward to, so I allowed the door to close behind me.

'Why did you close the door?'

This threw me. So, I answered as my autistic soul wanted me to – 'because it is heavy.' I then explained the problem. By this point, he had made me feel so uncomfortable that I didn't move any closer to the desk.

'Who will pay?'

I had no idea and said as such.

'Are we meant to bill the artists?' he sneered.

I had no answer and felt close to tears. I thanked him and left.

Even now I can't believe I thanked him, but it is one of the rules. I live my life by rules. My parents realised that I couldn't make quick decisions in social situations, so I had rules. One rule was to always be polite. Thank the man glowering in front of me for making me cry and basically telling me that there was no way I could do what I wanted because I was not a 'proper' student.

My supervisor caught me on the way out. He explained that the head guy had just had his funding cut. I guess it hit me then that no matter where I would go, I would always be at the bottom of the rung. I vowed there and then to never go back into research.

In the end, my dissertation was about my business; breeding rabbits for the pet market, something I had done since I was fourteen. It got me outside and I was able to sit in the sun for most of the summer playing with rabbits and creating artwork. If not for that conversation in the Doc's room, I think my future would have been very different. If I had got the funding, then my artwork would have been an abstract riot of colour and the data analysis would have been full of numbers and charts. Instead, I showed the inside of a rabbit nest, new-born kits and my analysis were full of animal behaviour and genetics. I probably would not have continued along the same path, although where I would have ended up is just a guess – quite possibly staring into a microscope somewhere.

I had a module, a palaeontology one. The lecturer had clocked that I had an analytical mind and that I was one of those kids who could do a puzzle with the grey backboard facing me. So, one day he placed a box in front of me.

'Sort that, would you?'

I opened it and saw a set of bones. Quickly getting them out of their packaging I put them together. It took me less than half an hour. He was surprised to see the reconstructed pterodactyl wing sitting on the bench and me back to the research I was reading. No words were exchanged, and he never thanked me. In hindsight, my unusual nature may have seemed aloof and unapproachable, but then he never tried. Surely, he must have been curious.

I still have trouble with being normal in conversations but then it was worse, I would simply blurt out facts. My random ask of 'can I do a PhD?' was met with stony silence and then a very cynical 'you can do what you want if you pay for it.' Then he left. I was still working out if that was a no. I decided in my autistic brain that it must have been a no, and in a few sentences the man who has also had issues with funding alters the path my life is taking. That was the last dinosaur bone I ever held. Perhaps, if I had known then I would have taken my time and not rushed the job. Later in life, I had the opportunity to study dinosaur footprints, but this was the last bone. Part of me wishes I had pursued it and had the experience of lifting a dinosaur from the ground, rock, dust and mud, but that was not to be.

My grade in university was not great, partially due to my dyslexia, with help arriving one week after my last exam. Help that was desperately needed. One exam I didn't realise that you must turn the exam paper over. My degree left me in the job centre.

I walked in and told them I have dyslexia and you could see the panic as they try to find something for me to do. Eventually one man asked if I liked conservation work.

'I did a module in that,' I said.

And that was my future set. I was enrolled onto an NVQ and sent to the local wildlife group. When I arrived, they were equally stumped about what to do with me.

At that time, I also asked my GP if I ought to get help because of my learning difficulties and he categorically said no, I was too high functioning. Instead of help, I was shunted to the local wildlife centre – something they did a lot with those they saw as a little special.

I loved the outside, so walking and helping in the wild was never a problem. The NVQ I could understand. I love to learn so filling out forms and doing tasks in order to get ticks was good. My writing was difficult to understand, but the teachers persevered. No one thought I had a degree. I was just someone a bit special. And I didn't mention the degree, I was tired of being kicked.

In the early morning I would walk the outdoor classroom path through the trees until the buzz from the electric station was not more than a minor hum in the background. It would be so quiet that a bee going about his business could be heard. The soft pops as I walked the bark filled path, past the tree that leaned on another, to the circle of stumps and logs. This would be where you opened the classroom. Onto the area we would get the children and teachers to build shelters and around to the end of the trail with plenty of hidey holes for a treasure hunt. The woodland was mostly conifers and larch with a few natives. The air would hum with life. Birds would sing and flowers were growing along the path. If not for that walk I don't think I would have coped. The rest of my time would be taken up with drawing. The wildlife company had to produce a biodiversity project for the council. I had over 153 illustrations to create. Really, they got an excellent deal as I didn't get paid a penny for it, except the benefits, which I could have received by not doing any work at all.

I walked the path and was happy in that moment.

After that I got a job that took me along coastal walks where I could enjoy the wind in my face and the smell of the sea. I smiled as I told people to pick up their dogs' shit. I carried bags for those who didn't have any. People seemed to like me. I needed structure in my days, or I would have fallen apart. Later, I got another job nearer to home and I swapped the seaweed and the damp sand for the woodland of a reclaimed slag heap in the midlands. I did it because I was told it was the next step. *You have a career*, people would say. If I could walk in the open air I didn't care. It was the one thing keeping me sane; from the biting cold of winter to the soft scent of spring and the heaviness of a humid summer, that was my love. Except that the higher I climbed on the job ladder, the less I saw of the outside. I made mistakes. My brain is not good at organising or keeping time. Hell, I can't tell time. So, it was something I was bound to fail. I was living my life as a lie. No one had any idea I was so depressed. Everything became literal. My mind shut itself into a black and white world. I basically did what I was told. My brain had become a simple processing engine. Consequently, when someone asked me to move some bales of hay, I didn't question the size or if they were being realistic, I simply got a wheelbarrow and went. A colleague went with me, who had started at the same time as me and was doing the same job.

'They asked us to move them?' she questioned.

I said yes. We found the bales; they were the large ones. I'm sure you have seen them. They are round and big, normally lifted by large machines, not two girls with wheelbarrows. By using physics and leverage I got the bales into the wheelbarrows and then we pushed them slowly into position. I made sure that I did all the lifting. Strangely, I was aware of the danger to my colleague but not to myself.

Later I went to the gym.

That night I woke screaming. An ambulance was called, and I had scans. I had trapped a nerve in my neck. The pain was unlike anything I had ever felt.

Suddenly and overnight, I was denied the outside. There were no more walks because any movement caused me pain. I was given a lump sum and a handshake, and the job vanished. I felt relief. And I learnt a lesson. A career might give a good wage, but if you lose the thing that you love in that job, it wasn't worth it.

I asked the doctors what I need to do to recover, and they said it was just time. I needed over a year.

A year.

I pottered to begin with. I got bored. I looked at my prospects and saw more of the same in the jobs I would get. And I said no.

Without the outside I had no wish to be in conservation and the jobs that gave you the outside did not give a living wage. My parents asked if I wanted to move with them. Up until that point it was assumed that I would stay in the Midlands whilst they moved to Wales. I thought of the caravan that I'd spent all summer, every summer in on the Llyn Peninsula and I didn't hesitate. Yes. That was it. I looked at the jobs around, but nothing jumped out at me. I was stuck.

Then I noticed the smallest university in the UK. It was only half an hour away from the new house and it had a course I wished I had done originally. Archaeology. The perfect balance between research and outside. I went to the interview and the lecturer told me that he didn't think I would finish, but I was in. A mature student. I was walking in the sun again.

This time I handed over my dyslexia report and set up help immediately. My life had a purpose. I brought a trowel and waited to be introduced to mud and bones. This time I didn't push my head above the pulpit. I kept everything on an even keel. I studied and had fun with friends. I sat on the grass and healed. Ultimately my path wasn't set in the world of the archaeologist; my head for the fine detail meant that I was steered toward the microscope and the lab. I had no wish to be there so when the decision came to follow the career I smiled and walked away.

If not for the bale of hay I guess I would have carried on in my previous job and probably become a teacher, although a bad one. More than likely, I would have had some sort of breakdown. By lifting that bale, I changed my life, and rather than withdrawing from the environment I walked further toward it. The archaeology degree taught me I am pretty good at it, but I am excellent at telling stories. Now I sit in a study that is surrounded by plants. I have a back garden filled with vegetables. A park that means I can walk in the country but live in a city. I no longer simply walk in nature; I exist in it.

Due to my colour and my disability, I have never really belonged, but the strange thing is that nature doesn't care. It simply is. The fact that I can still get outside everyday means I am balanced. Archaeology taught me how to create a story from something as small as an arrowhead. Without the accident I could not have done it, because I would never have looked. I would simply have existed and mourned the loss of the freedom I had as a conservation warden on a piece of land. Now I can write where I want, even if that is the garden, a park or inside. The green goes with me.

Image description: black and white illustration of a tree overlooking a grave which has flowers growing from it.

From God We Come and To God We Return

DR SOFIA REHMAN

Muslims are encouraged when they find themselves in any kind of loss or difficulty to recite the words;

إِنَّا لِلهِ وَإِنَّـا إِلَيْهِ رَاجِعونَ

'Indeed, from God we come and to God it is that we return.' These are words I recited fervently and almost continually in the summer of 2021 when my father suddenly passed away. The words became a way of grounding myself, a sort of proverbial anchor when I could feel myself unmooring, setting adrift in the turmoil of grief and the unforeseeable ruptures that emerged from the loss of my dad. My dad, the man I looked upon as a mountain. I always thought him invincible and fearless, undefeatable, not even by death. The Qur'an describes mountains as pegs[1] that stabilise the earth[2] and that is what I realised my dad had been in my life; a stabilising force in his quiet but monumental way.

---

1 Surah al-Naba 78:7
2 Surah al-Nahl 16:15

My first love of the great outdoors was instilled in me by him. He wasn't by any means a particularly involved father, but in the times that he was fully present with his children, he shaped us with and connected and rooted us to the things he loved, foremost amongst them his love of nature and the wild. So as we lowered him into the ground, the July rain gently falling as a mercy from the sky, the leaves of the tree under which he was being buried rustling a soothing chorus of hushes like a mother settling her child to bed, the moment didn't overwhelm me as I had thought it would. Instead, I could see the physical lowering of my father into the ground was only corporeal, on a metaphysical level the soul was ascending into another space of serenity. Again, I uttered the words, from God we come and to God we return. It struck me then that when we come into this world from God, it is through the womb and when we return to God, it is through the earth: women and the earth, both portals to and from the Divine and yet both so utterly exploited and subjugated by the greed and tyranny of men.

In the days that followed my dad's passing, comfort came in many forms; the cup of tea my best friend made when we got home from the hospital that evening, my children's embrace, and our neighbours' pots of food to name a few. But an unexpected comfort were the birds from my dad's devotionally tended garden. Many times, I would step outside to find a little bird land on my shoulder, follow me around the garden, and chirp at me until I sat down on the grass from where it would proceed to jump onto my knee and then onto my head. Sometimes there would be the fearless bird who would hop right over the threshold of the French doors of my parents' home and stride right into the living room.

In my work on gender justice in Islam, a guiding principle is the Tawhidic paradigm conceptualised by the scholar Amina Wadud. Tawhid in Islam is the concept of the unicity of God;

not only the Oneness of God but also the unifying nature of God. In her book, *Inside the Gender Jihad*, Wadud argues that through the principle defining attribute of Islam – *tawhid* – Muslims can strive for and realise an ordering of the world that is just and based on mercy and compassion. She further states that establishing such a social order is the very purpose for which humans were created as khalīfas, vicegerents of God. This social order, she asserts, engenders a reciprocity between the creation of God before God; a dismantling of unjust hierarchies, whilst also allowing direct connection to God for each individual regardless of their corporeal realities. Based on this understanding of tawhid, Wadud develops the Tawhidic paradigm whereby inter-human interactions are presented as taking place within a triad where all peoples are in a horizontal relationship of reciprocity while God occupies a transcendent space above in a way that sustains the relationship of equality and mutual responsibility between all humans.

Through this paradigm, we are reminded that all peoples before Allah are equal; that no person or group of people are considered superior to another on the basis of class, race, ethnicity, gender, sexuality, or any other mode of division. Any disruption to the order of equality and mutual reciprocity established by the tawhidic paradigm is a break from the establishment of this foundational principle in the establishment of Islam. And yet here we are. Women remain embattled in an ongoing fight against patriarchal oppressions, not least in terms of maternal health and bodily autonomy. In 2021, it was widely reported that in the UK Black women are four times more likely than white women to die in childbirth and that Black and Asian British babies have a more than 50% higher risk of perinatal mortality, compared to white British babies.[3] If it

---

3   *National Maternity & Perinatal Audit.* maternityaudit.org.uk.

is from God that we come into the world through the womb, then we are clearly failing in our purpose of establishing mercy and compassion around this Divine entry point.

And if it is through the earth that we return to God, then this Divine exit point has also been catastrophically failed. Historically, humans saw themselves as one with the universe around them. Muslim intellectual heritage is filled with odes to the oneness of human existence with all that is around it, particularly nature and an understanding that we are part of nature; it is not separate from us. After my dad passed, I found life decided to throw multiple curve balls at me. Concerned for my mental health, my husband and children arranged a summer spent by the sea or at the Lakes. In my return to the water, I found freedom, lightness and sanctuary. The waves playfully tossed me to shore, awakening the child still within me. The lakes provided a calm stillness to step into, reinstating equilibrium and harmony. Water plays a pivotal role in storytelling in Islam, unsurprising when the arid desert lands of Arabia are recalled as the birthplace of Islam. Shari'ah, now so misunderstood and much maligned, but which essentially refers to Islamic law, also means 'the path to a watering hole'. In other words, the laws of Islam are supposed to be a means to delivering those who believe, to actions, norms and regulations which give life and allow all of creation to flourish. Likewise, water is often a metaphor for knowledge. The Qur'an refers to revelation as descending from the heavens. The Arabic word *nazala/anzala* نزل\انزل is used to describe the descent of revelation from the heavens to earth, and of water from the sky to the earth. The former is a life source for our souls and the latter for our bodies. But for water to be pure once on earth, it needs to remain in action; still, water becomes stagnant, impure. Likewise, for Divine knowledge to remain relevant to the lives of twenty-first century believers, it must also stay dynamic, actions must flow from it.

An oft-repeated instruction in the Qur'an is for each person to look to the natural world around them not only to marvel at its wonders but to contemplate its many lessons. The daily prayers of the Muslim are set by the cyclical motion of the sun through the sky; a continual reminder of our interconnectivity with all around us. However, much of this relationship was severed ironically by Enlightenment philosophers and then imported and violently imposed through colonialism. Earlier in 2022, the International Panel on Climate Change (IPCC)'s report on the impact of global warming asserted for the first time in its history the ongoing effects of colonialism on climate change, acknowledging the vulnerability of particular people and places to the impacts of climate change as a direct result of colonial legacy.[4] In September 2022, the country of my heritage, Pakistan, experienced record-breaking floods with over 33 million people affected, 1.7 million homes destroyed, almost 2,000 people killed and vast amounts of damage done to infrastructure.[5] It was acknowledged at the time that the increase in monsoon rains that led to this climate disaster was likely to have been 'made up to 50% worse by global heating'. But this is not a one-off event. Climate change has resulted in floods, extreme heatwaves, and cyclones. The unsustainable rate at which capitalism drives us to further plunder the earth's resources and pollute it without regard has created a new global apartheid. Climate justice activist, Asad Rehman said at the closing of COP26, 'The rich have refused to do their fair share, more empty words on climate

---

4 "Colonialism: why leading climate scientists have finally acknowledged its link with climate change." Harriet Mercer, *The Conversation*. 22 April 2022. theconversation.com/colonialism-why-leading-climate-scientists-have-finally-acknowledged-its-link-with-climate-change-181642.
5 "Pakistan floods 'made up to 50% worse by global heating.'" Fiona Harvey, *The Guardian*. 15 September 2022. theguardian.com/environment/2022/sep/15/pakistan-floods-made-up-to-50-worse-by-global-heating

finance. You have turned your backs on the poorest who face a crisis of COVID, economic and climate apartheid because of the actions of the richest. It is immoral for the rich to talk about the future of their children and grandchildren when the children of the Global South are dying now.'[6]

As Fanon so eloquently described, to be colonised is to be dehumanised, made inferior and racialised as Other. It is to be part of the 'collateral damage' of the hyper consumerism and rush to accumulate that capitalism has fostered. Climate coloniality is an extension and continuation of the colonial legacy. It haunts previously colonised countries through the climate-induced disasters that continue to be visited disproportionately on the Global South. The Global South which was plundered of its resources through colonial invasions, and left underdeveloped and resource-poor, while the Global North benefitted from its resources and became not only developed, but overdeveloped. This legacy continues through neo-colonialism in our present times. Rob Nixon referred to a 'slow violence'[7] resulting from climate change which has allowed deaths, devastations, marginalisation and increased vulnerabilities to go unremarked upon, but the impact has gained critical mass and cannot be ignored any longer.

Capitalism, gone wild on the insatiable hunger of corporate greed has unleashed an unprecedented corruption upon the earth. In the Qur'an,

ظَهَرَ ٱلْفَسَادُ فِى ٱلْبَرِّ وَٱلْبَحْرِ بِمَا كَسَبَتْ أَيْدِى ٱلنَّاسِ لِيُذِيقَهُم بَعْضَ ٱلَّذِى عَمِلُواْ لَعَلَّهُمْ يَرْجِعُونَ

---

6   Farhana Sultana, "The unbearable heaviness of climate coloniality," *Political Geography*, Volume 99, 2022,102638, ISSN 0962-6298, doi.org/10.1016/j.polgeo.2022.102638.

7   *Slow Violence and the Environmentalism of the Poor*, Rob Nixon. Harvard University Press, 2013.

'Corruption has spread on land and sea as a result of what people's hands have done, that He may make them taste a part of what they have done so that they might return [to the Right Path]'[8]

Islam is a religion that promotes hope. Despite the dark turn we have taken, and the frightening consequences of climate change wrought on the earth's most vulnerable communities due to the colonial matrix of racism, patriarchy and capitalism, none of these are insurmountable problems. These are human-made problems, a corruption brought about by 'what people's hands have done', and if people's hands have brought us to this disaster, the people's hands can also dismantle the structures that have delivered us to this point and rebuild a world with fair and equal distribution of wealth and resources, that rotates on the axis of mercy, justice and compassion. We can actively pursue anti-racist, anti-capitalist, and eco-friendly lifestyles, lobby, protest and organise. We can and must raise our consciousness and see that the disasters that happen 'over there' are only days away from happening over here too. That we cannot turn a blind eye to the suffering of the world's most vulnerable, deluded by the idea that we are safe from the earth's anguish.

Often taught to Muslim children for its brevity and melody, is the 99th chapter of the Qur'an, *Surah al-Zalzalah*, The Earthquake. It is one that is regularly pondered by Muslim adults. It states:

إِذَا زُلْزِلَتِ ٱلْأَرْضُ زِلْزَالَهَا

When the earth is shaken to her (utmost) convulsion

وَأَخْرَجَتِ ٱلْأَرْضُ أَثْقَالَهَا

And the earth throws up her burdens (from within)

---

8   Qur'an 30:41

وَقَالَ ٱلْإِنسَـٰنُ مَا لَهَا

And man cries (distressed): 'What is the matter with her?'

يَوْمَئِذٍ تُحَدِّثُ أَخْبَارَهَا

On the Day she will declare her tidings:

بِأَنَّ رَبَّكَ أَوْحَىٰ لَهَا

On that Day your Lord will have given her inspiration

يَوْمَئِذٍ يَصْدُرُ ٱلنَّاسُ أَشْتَاتًا لِّيُرَوْا أَعْمَـٰلَهُ

On that Day will men then proceed in companies sorted out,
to be shown the deeds that they (had done).

فَمَن يَعْمَلْ مِثْقَالَ ذَرَّةٍ خَيْرًا يَرَهُ

Then shall anyone who has done an atoms weight of good,
see it!

وَمَن يَعْمَلْ مِثْقَالَ ذَرَّةٍ شَرًّا يَرَهُ

And anyone who has done an atoms weight of evil,
shall see it.

Normative readings of this chapter will relate its message
to the Day of Resurrection, but Islamic theologian, Rabia Terri
Harris suggests an additional way of reading it; one in which we
can see the scene described in the chapter as playing out right
now before our very eyes. She urgently implores readers to ask
themselves, in today's world don't we see the earth convulsing?
And in response aren't people bewildered and asking, 'What
is the matter with her?' Every day our news feeds deliver to
us news of another forest fire, another drought, another flood,
another earthquake. Isn't this the earth screaming its message

to us? Isn't this the very 'inspiration' God warns They will grant the earth by which it will communicate with us? Harris goes on to draw our attention to the word used by God in this chapter to describe the earth's speech as being awha اوحى, and that this word is from the Arabic word, wahy وحى, meaning revelation as revealed to prophets. She argues then that the 'speech' of the earth is as authoritative as the speech of prophets; both inspired by the Divine with words of Truth. That being the case, to ignore the earth and its call, is as grave as ignoring the call of the prophets.[9]

To heed the earth's call, we need to heal the rupture between us and the earth, the natural world around us, and of course, one another. Science and data alone will not save us – we need an ethics of care and reconnection to nature. This does not mean we all need to be Muslim or even religious, but we must recover those ethics and beliefs that once did this in order to learn from and reconnect through the guidance they provide. It is from God that we come, and to God that we return, let our time on this earth be one of honouring this space and one another.

---

9   "This Speaking Earth." Rabia Terri Harris, in *The Women's Khutbah Book: Contemporary Sermons on Spirituality and Justice from around the World*, Sa'diyya Shaikh, Fatima Seedat. Yale University Press, 2023, pp.59-60.

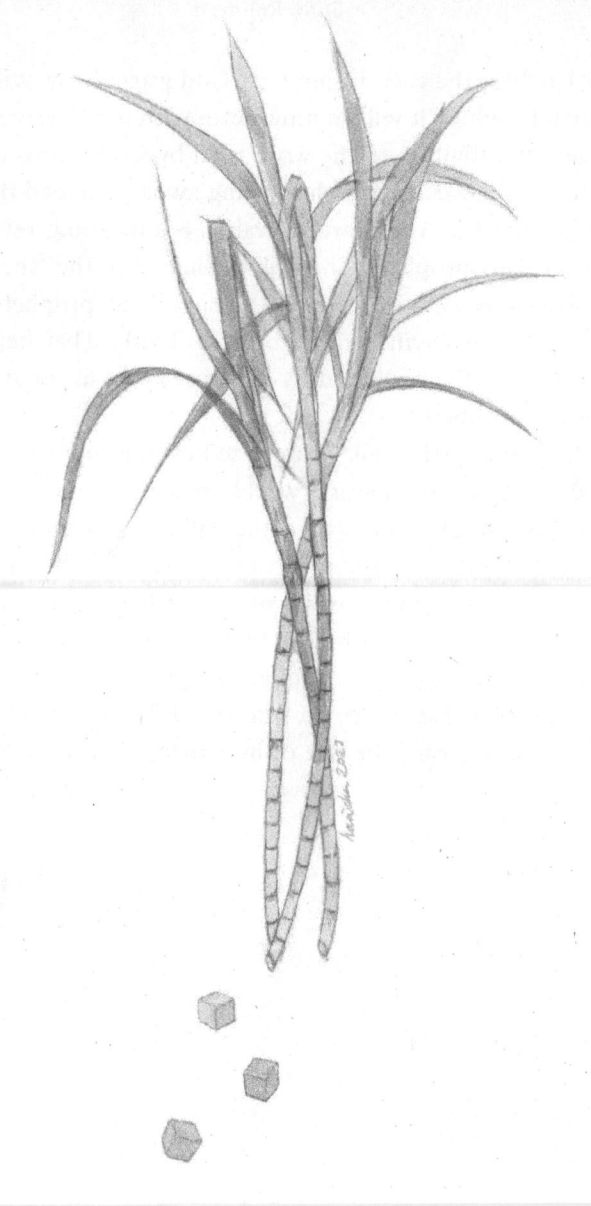

Image description: black and white illustration of sugar cane, with sugar cubes below it.

In a Relationship
with Sugar

MAYA CHOWDHRY

This is an interactive essay – participation is optional.

To take part, get your phone, and a piece of any sweet substance you have to hand; jelly babies, chocolate, a sugar cube, ready.

Not ready? Then let your eyes flick over the black ink on white paper and imagine you are participating.

Ready?

Scan this QR code.

As the first part of the track plays, please taste your sweet substance, slowly savouring how it awakens your tastebuds. Then, as the second track plays, continue to relish your sweet something. In your mind, note any differences between your eating experience during track one and track two.

Now the theory.

> Babies respond to sweetness
> by sticking their tongue out,
> and to bitterness by retracting it.

Brown or white?

I mean sugar. But I could mean babies, it's part of the same story. Sugar is one of those foodstuffs that illustrate our human relationship to food and food justice in a way that few other substances do. The history of its production and consumption has not only changed the biology of humans but epitomises human cultural changes over 500 years, as the trading of sugar resulted in transatlantic slavery and capitalism.

> Sugar—or rather, the great commodity market which arose demanding it—has been one of the massive demographic forces in world history. Because of it, literally millions of enslaved Africans reached the New World, particularly the American South, the Caribbean and its littorals, the Guianas and Brazil.[1]

---

1   *Sweetness and Power: The Place of Sugar in Modern History*, Sidney Mintz. New York, NY: Viking, 1985, p. 71

Interactions

In recent years, my interdisciplinary creative practice has focused on live art – in particular live art where the participant and their interactions are the focus of the art. I became interested in this type of practice as I feel it breaks down the boundaries of what art is, and how art is situated in the world, i.e. no separation between art and life, life and art. This essay asks you to both participate beyond reading and thinking, and to blur the boundaries between essay, story and art.

My work exploring food justice came about from exploring the materiality of my themes: I was making a piece about world water scarcity, and I wanted there to be actual water in the piece. I came across sonic seasoning when I was using chocolate to create an artwork and wanted to incorporate the idea of sensory modalities in an embodied way. I was introduced to commensality, the act of eating together, when I created 'What's Eating Reality', an immersive dining experience. The creation of this artwork brought full circle my journey from chef to artist.

A spun sugar basket I made in catering college was the centrepiece of our annual banquet. In this educational establishment we were taught that the melting point of sugar crystals was 160°C, that 10–20 degrees more and it caramelises because of atoms and molecules moving faster. But we were never taught about what Mintz[2] refers to as 'sugared emblems', elaborate edible displays through which royalty and nobility boasted of their wealth, and that epitomised colonialism.

When I was an eleven-year-old kid visiting India for the first time, our grandparents tried to give us *Tate & Lyle* white sugar to

---

2   Ibid, p. 89

sprinkle on our breakfast parathas. My dad rejected this colonial legacy and got us the best Indian sweetmeats, jaggery and sugar cane juice from the street vendor in Lajpat Nagar market, thus welcoming us to our cultural heritage. Jaggery, an unrefined sugar with an earthy, almost gritty taste, has existed in India for over 5,000 years both as a sweetener and as an Ayurvedic medicine – retaining nutrients that refined sugar depletes.

Sugar, or sucrose $(C_{12}H_{22}O_{11})$, is manufactured photosynthetically by green plants. We humans can't make sugar. The best we can do is to extract it, and change its form. We have been doing so zealously, for more than 2,000 years.[3]

Fast forward and I've abandoned catering collage, with its misogynistic and racist culture, for activist art. I'm in my artist studio. I've spent the last 30 minutes distractedly reading a *ScienceDirect* article about the health benefits of jaggery; for instance, it is digested more slowly than refined sugar and as such releases energy at a slower rate. It also contains anti-oxidants associated with anti-aging. I type 'where can you buy jaggery in Manchester' and the photographs transport me to the point that I'm salivating with memories of the sugar cane juice we drunk as kids in India; I spend another 30 minutes trying to find out if you can buy sugar cane here. I hate G**gle, it swallows my dreams.

Sometime later I find myself sitting at my picnic table back in my art studio. In front of me are six types of sugar; agave syrup, molasses, jaggery, white sugar lumps, golden syrup and raw cane sugar. There's a small amount on each teaspoon. I'm testing out something I read on the internet whilst searching

---

3   "Sugar." Sidney Mintz. sidneymintz.net/sugar.php

for sugarcane stockists, an article from Oxford University no less. It's alluding to higher frequencies resulting in sweeter tastes being reported and lower frequencies being more bitter, and it sounds a trifle far fetched. There are some graphs in the article I can't decipher, but something about them draws me in. I'm approaching this article with art, not science, looking for a lens to approach the experience of eating sugar and what it tells us about food vs an analysis of the properties of sugar and what the body does/not do when consuming it. In art I'm not trying to prove any of the latter, instead I adopt a 'knowledge creation through making' approach and allow the facts to wash over me and infuse as I create.

I press play and a track booms out from a little Bluetooth speaker, *dfff dfff dmmm dmmm*.

I open a sachet of white sugar, tip it onto the teaspoon, and pour it on my tongue. The granules instantly dissolve, then I close my mouth. I experience a warm sticky feeling. I feel fed. A head rush. I am not accustomed to eating sugar!

I can't resist the memories flung up by my neurons and I'm instantly transported to 1974, where we four kids are in the kitchen after school. My brother slathers some Mother's Pride white sliced bread with Stork margarine, and then sprinkles on copious amounts of white sugar, and sandwiches it into his mouth. The crystals crunch between his teeth.

Weird, it doesn't taste as sweet as I expected it would.

By the way how did your sugary item taste with track one? Sweet? Bitter?

I rinse my mouth out with diluted lemon juice, take a swig of water, and lick the molasses of the teaspoon.

Even less sweet. Even after the acidity of the lemon juice. Lemon justice.

My typo is interesting.

I return to the graph in the article, squint at its contours, the x and y axes. Read the narrative explaining the experiment at the Crossmodal Research Laboratory at Oxford University by psychologist Professor Charles Spence. Although this is fledgling research, they have yet to discover the theory's mechanisms by which frequencies affect taste. I am not surprised that, although they have proved this occurs in the lab, they still don't know why. All of our senses can potentially contribute to how we perceive taste, resulting in a very individual response, combined with our unique biology – complex sounds can be perceived in different ways due to both how our brains process the sounds and factors such as the shape and position of our ears.

> In one of the earliest sonic seasoning studies, Crisinel et al. (2012) demonstrated that a bittersweet cinder toffee could be sonically seasoned to taste either a little sweeter or more bitter.[4]

* * *

Savouring the molasses, I am simultaneously transported to a Victorian kitchen, Hill Station in Darjeeling, and the pick 'n mix counter in a sweet shop in Edinburgh. Sweet memories rushing into the sugar stories that have melted me, left me with a bitter aftertaste of how sugar reached the shores of so-called Great Britain. How it was consumed, and shaped the bodies, minds and spirits of many generations through the brutal transatlantic slave trade. Sugar was one of the main commodities that literally fueled colonialism. It went from being a

---

4   Spence Charles, "Sonic Seasoning and Other Multisensory Influences on the Coffee Drinking Experience," *Frontiers in Computer Science*, Volume 3, 2021. frontiersin.org/articles/10.3389/fcomp.2021.644054

rare and expensive substance in Antiquity and the Middle Ages to being highly in demand by Europe and America in the fifteenth century. In an effort to fulfil this demand, and to make sugar more affordable, the colonisers violently enacted land grabs, and the enslavement of Africans on sugar plantations and the displacement of indigenous peoples. This is the same sugar that also fueled, as Yusoff discusses in *A Billion Black Anthropocenes or None*,[5] the English white working classes to extract coal and fuel the industrial revolution.

I think I'm having a sugar high, having consumed more sugar in one afternoon than I have in the last five years. I go into my kitchen, take down a recipe book from the shelf and begin making the puff candy we grew up on, that gave us energy to be children, and blackened our teeth.

Are you still savouring your sweet substance? Here we move on from sonic seasoning towards a pairing of sugar and poetry. Taste and read:

* * *

Sugar and I met in the Turkish delights
my sister and I made as kids,
icing sugar was white as snow, shiny, silky,
dissolved your tongue into smiles.

We marvelled and delighted at how brown sugar liquified
from its crystals into sweet syrup,
how it disappeared into butter making creamy fudge.

---

5 *A Billion Black Anthropocenes or None*, Kathryn Yusoff. Minneapolis, MN: University of Minnesota Press, 2018.

Sugar was transformation.

Meanwhile sugar's tall cane-like greenish-violet grasses
sway in the warm wet breeze of a plantation in Gujarat.
The rough, rasping, saw-toothed edges of its leaves
greet the air in symbiotic breath.

Sugar was what we had for lunch,
spending our dinner money on Snickers and bubblegum.

Sugar accompanied our homework
sprinkled on buttery toasted sugar sandwiches.

Sugar and me were formally introduced in history and biology,
condensed versions of the violence of English colonialism,
and how sugar could give energy to my cells, dopamine to my brain.

I loved sugar for its sweet memories of fairy cakes with
    butterfly wings
treacle sponge pudding and ice-cream sundaes.
All would be bereft without sugar.

But I didn't love the granulated history of Tate and Lyle,
    its white crystals stained red with the blood of enslaved
    humans on Caribbean plantations.

So white sugar and I went our separate ways and
    I baked with molasses caring for my body whilst trying to
    eat in a fairer way.

But sugar made me crash and burn,
and that's when I discovered sugar was not for me.

* * *

I'm neither a scientist – unlike the majority of my family – nor an anthropologist or a historian. I return to the only experimentation I know. I turn away from sugar molecules back to art to explore my relationship with sugar, and sugar's relationship with food justice. Sugar was a cheap source of energy for workers during the industrial revolution, as were refined carbohydrates, but these foodstuffs were low in nutrients. Food justice is defined as humans having access to affordable and healthy food – food production and distribution as part of the industrial complex has resulted in low quality food produced for profit. This is only part of the story of our relationship with sugar, because it is not only about access to foodstuffs, it's about education to make informed choices about how and when sugar is detrimental to your health.

I continue eating sugar augmented with different frequencies to look sugar in the eye. To feel how and why humans have been bitterly consumed with this plant, substance, foodstuffs, for centuries, despite our knowledge that its creation has caused so much bitter suffering.

* * *

10,000 Hz is the frequency at which sugar dissolves on the tongue

174 Hz is the frequency at which we are told sugar is bad for us.
Is it pleasure they mean?
or the tooth decay?

9,000 Hz is the frequency at which we are told we are responsible for our own health,

despite our genes
don't eat too much fat,
no, we mean don't eat carbs,
no, we mean don't eat sugar
Really mean it this time
Don't eat sugar!

3,000 Hz is the frequency of despair at being told to reduce
sugar out of your diet to seven sugar cubes a day
Which means if you take sugar in your tea or coffee
Then
. No jam, no fizzy drinks, no Frosties
And there's an essay on the NHS website to help you work this
out from any packaged food
It says:
'Watch out for other words used to describe the sugars added
to food and drinks, such as
cane sugar, honey, brown sugar,
high-fructose corn syrup,
fruit juice concentrate/purées,
corn syrup,
fructose, sucrose, glucose, crystalline sucrose,
nectars, blossom,
maple and agave syrups,
dextrose, maltose, molasses and treacle.'

I mean who even has time to read food labels, even if you
could understand what they mean for your health and longevity
– nutraceuticals, a term for foods which aid the prevention or
treatment of disease, are mainly a marketing ploy.

99 Hz is the frequency of despair at trying to understand how
much sugar you can safely eat.

Brownian noise (its change in sound signal/frequency from one moment to the next is random) is the frequency of dejection when you realise 'Fairtrade' is just a label and a hogshead of sugar is a colonial barrel that has been rolling though the lives of Black and Brown people forever.

In my mind's eye, I fade out the sound by turning an imaginary dial. I fade out the sound so I can have a moment to reflect on the thought above.

Why make art, why not campaign for food justice? Why not do both? What are the different processes by which we read and absorb, listen, and absorb? Find out. Feel our way to justice. Take action.

I continually return to art from activism to devise an experience that allows an audience to expand their explorations of their relationship with food, their relationship with food justice. And I wonder why I find eating sugar traumatic, when those around me don't seem to mind. Or they don't say they mind.

This experience seeks conversations, mind wanderings, thoughts that congeal like melting jelly babies, seeking a way to consider how I am in a relationship with sugar, and how you are in a relationship with sugar and how we can work together so that the 's' of sugar and the 't' of trade make sugar cane juice into justice we drink together.

Reach out, put your sweet substance in the palm of your hand (or imagine yourself doing this) as you look down at the sweet something; sugar cube, jelly babies, chocolate, reflect on why we humans need sweetness, need bitter tastes, on how we can balance our needs and desires. Choose to eat or not.

Image description: black and white illustration of a woman with long dark hair playing guitar underneath a tree.

I am Punk by Nature

NADIA JAVED

Punk is my home
Punk is my space
Punk is the little girl with a brown face
Punk is my heart
Punk from the start
Punk was my voice when I didn't have a choice

I am a British Indian/Pakistani working-class girl. I grew up in Hayes, in Middlesex, and served as the front woman of all-female, all-punk band The Tuts from age 15 to 30, until we disbanded in 2019. To paint a picture of my astrological profile, I have a Cancer sun, Scorpio moon, and Virgo rising. This means I am sensitive, fierce, creative and all these amazing qualities make me who I am, it makes me overly emotional and fall into toxic cycles. It's intense. During my childhood, I was obsessed with nineties pop and the Spice Girls. As a young teenager, I transitioned to punk pop and indie music, and admired bands primarily fronted by white men.

Punk was a world created where me and my best friend Bev could do what we wanted, where we could be confident and unapologetic, wear unconventional clothes, fight the Tories, fight for social justice and equality. Punk gave me the confidence of all those white men I admired in youth. Punk bands were my religion, and rock stars were my idols. Punk gave me hope and provided me with something to channel energy towards. It was inspiring and gave permission to be whoever I wanted to be. It allowed me to create my own reality. Punk became a new home for me, where I could finally say, *Fuck you, I'm not scared. I'm fearless, I'm enough, I'm talented, and I don't care about what people think of me. I'm just being myself.*

I'm now known as a Muslim punk, and I'm proud to be Muslim and punk. For me, the two aren't in conflict. In fact, I think it's honouring God to be punk. The best songs find me and write themselves, as if I'm a vessel being used by God to get a message out. Punk allowed me to speak my truth, allowing a force of nature within me to break free. Nature and punk aren't far from one another, as nature, too, does whatever it wants.

Growing up in Hayes, there was never much nature around. Back in those days, Hayes was considered countryside but my only interaction with nature was either in my garden or school trips to Kew gardens. As a kid I didn't really think about nature or our lack of access to it. To me, nature was the park, the swings, playing on the grass, kicking a football in the garden or running around on the field at school. It wouldn't be until my thirties that I would begin to understand what nature could mean to me.

At the beginning of my punk journey, I wasn't aware of the terms 'Riot Grrrl' or 'intersectional feminism', nor even the lack of representation for people of colour in the scene. I didn't foresee how we'd have to work ten times harder than the white men of punk to gain commercial success. Even though I never saw pop or rock stars who looked like me, that didn't deter my desire to pursue a music career. I, along with my best friends

Beverley Ishmael and Harriet Doveton, formed The Tuts through which I rose to prominence and used my platform to speak out, taking up space in an industry dominated by white guys. We secured major tours with artists like Kate Nash, played at Glastonbury, and toured with two-tone legends like The Selecter and The Specials, as well as Riot Grrrl pioneers Bikini Kill. Everyone knew the fun we were having as I would constantly update social media with hilarious Instagram stories of our outfits, us throwing money around like rappers and mocking men at the merch, and with photos on the Insta grid and vlogs on YouTube.

However, in the end, nature catches up with you. In December 2018, we found ourselves burned out. The Tuts broke up. How did we transition from being so authentically punk and aligned to our sudden disbandment? The following year also marked the end of my eight year long relationship with my boyfriend. The dissolution of my band and losing the stability of my long-term relationship made it hard to regulate my emotions. It may have been the most significant heartbreak of my life (the band that was). Perhaps that, too, was part of the natural process.

There was no longer a shield I could hide behind, neither my band nor my guitar. I didn't have a stable boyfriend to soothe me either. There were no more merch tables to engage and entertain fans. Our fans ranged from young girls to older men. We empowered the former and playfully took money from the latter, who seemed to sweat and foam from the mouth in excitement, reacting to our teasing. But now, my ability to express myself and connect with others through music had vanished. I didn't have anything real to post on social media, and the truth felt too vulnerable to share, especially since we hadn't officially announced the split and still haven't. I had always felt born to be onstage, but the band that had once been my saviour had faded away, and it was time to let go and try and become a solo artist that deep down I wanted and knew I could succeed in – but I stood in my own way. The cycle had completed, and it was now time to face up as my skin shed and leaves fell, bleeding from the branches of my broken heart.

My purpose, identity and anchor felt stripped from me and I was compelled to finally confront unresolved childhood trauma, including my struggles with co-dependency and abandonment issues. I was about ten years old when my parents got divorced. My mum worked tirelessly and my dad moved out by court order. That meant, for me, no rules, no boundaries, and I could pretty much do whatever I wanted. I spent a lot of time alone. Being home alone most evenings, my stomach churned as I felt trapped in my body, hoping for someone to soothe me. I was anxious without knowing why, and I didn't know how to ask for help. I was too young to understand what was going on with my mental health. Perhaps what I felt was shame to admit that I was not ok, a need to always be strong and brave and for everyone else to be okay. I was a child, I didn't know how to soothe myself but now, as an adult, it's my responsibility.

The move to secondary school was brutal. I did myself no favours by getting kicked out of class all the time. If I wasn't trying to make people laugh, I was fighting racists and bullies, who were all boys. They would call me all sorts of names for my skin colour and big ears. I made my life harder by answering back, cussing, and sticking up for myself. I was a rebel, and my inner punk refused to stay silent. In my primary school I was shy and now I'd done a full 180 from being timid to troublesome. Subconsciously, this made me the class clown.

At this time, I had no connection to nature, nor thought that it could be good for mental health. I didn't need it as much as others, maybe because I felt more grounded through creativity and performing. Through these troublesome school years, music and writing saved me and continues to today. Some of my favourite songs draw references from nature, like The Libertines' 'Don't Look Back Into the Sun'. The Libertines made it okay to not be perfect in musicianship, that you didn't need to be classically trained or able to read music to be charming and messy, to recklessly thrash a guitar with a sweaty face and leather jacket and move hundreds of thousands of people around the world. Feeling creative myself, I began to draw parallels between nature and my life experiences, looking for interesting ways of describing what was around me.

We don't need any back up
We don't need any back up
Because we are gonna bud and blossom
Spread our pollen to the people
Make our sound truly ripple
Cos our roots are in the ground

I wrote those lyrics on a walk to school. It was about breaking free. Flourishing and rising above. At the time, I didn't overthink it, letting it flow out as a freestyle. I called it 'Back Up', which would be played on BBC 6 Music by Iggy Pop years later. Looking back now, perhaps I was talking about the racists and the bullies. To 'blossom' was to break free from stereotypes and become a rock star. 'Pollen' was for my music to reach people far and wide – world domination, as I'd always say.

Once the band was gone, I could see the areas of myself that I needed to work on, the aspects I had never come to terms with. Success was about big wins, but now I realise the small victories are just as important. I embarked on a profound journey of introspection and self-discovery, going to Bali by myself and instigating a year-long hiatus from social media. What were once effortless social media posts were now plagued by doubt, leading to a cycle of posting and deleting. Seeking solace, I ventured outdoors, immersing myself in nature to calm my anxiety. As a Cancerian, a water sign, my need to be near water is innate, but I found a unique harmony between land and water. The rustling of leaves, the songs of birds, the vibrant green parakeets and red kites circling the sky, squirrels being squirrels, peaceful ponds all embraced me as I started going on walk in nature. All until I'd get pounced on by someone's dogs who sensed my anxiety as I waddled around in my ankle-length North Face coat. The owners didn't apologise as their dogs clawed muddy paws all over me. Nevertheless, I cherished the feeling of being invisible, an anonymous existence free from expectations and the weight of a digital audience, a weight I placed on myself.

Following my return from Bali, I loved going to Hampstead Heath, North London's popular green area. It's got trees, open spaces, a hill with a view of London, and lots of posh middle-class people with posh dogs. Familiarity grew with specific trees as I journalled from under my favourite one opposite the pond at Kenwood House. 'Earthing', the simple act of sitting on the ground and touching soil, has been proven to reduce inflammation in the body. Hours were spent wandering, accompanied by the melodies of Amy Winehouse. Amidst the trees, inhaling pure, non-polluted Heathrow airport air, I felt my nervous system rebalance but nothing would cure that deep underlying depressed feeling. The longing for love and validation. Being away from everyone, all the noise, all the distractions, and social media meant I could work on aspects of the self, self-love, self-worth and self-esteem. I would sit by the men's swimming lake, watching them while eating my overpriced cake from Gail's. I think there's too much emphasis on self-love and becoming hyper independent. I believe we can heal and grow in relationships and you don't necessarily have to have this all mastered before you enter one.

In London, it's hard to access quiet, green spaces. My commute to Hampstead Heath was long, involving the intolerable north circular. When the trip became too much, I started going to Black Park, a woodland near Slough. There, in the middle of nowhere, I would walk in the woods, listening to songs I'd recorded on my phone to check if they were any good, and engage in candid, heartfelt conversations with nature, talking out loud because I felt held and close to God. I'd cry to the trees, ask for help, blessings, guidance, and protection.

I used to mock the way white middle-class people dressed in their outdoor clothing and hiking boots, but now I am a proud owner of boots and merino wool socks from Mountain Warehouse. Nature has taught me that I can embrace all sides of myself, as nature doesn't try to be anything other than itself. In a world that conditions us to self-loathe, embracing oneself becomes an act of rebellion.

I now understand that validation and self-love must come from within. That no matter how many shows you play or fans you make, it won't fill a void. I'm incredibly proud of the progress I've made to recognise and embody that understanding. It doesn't mean I'm not an amazing frontwoman, and I still want to celebrate my ability to stand on stage, sing, tell stories, and captivate an audience. But I can't rely solely on that to sustain me. I need to have inner peace in knowing I am enough just as I am. But, fucking hell, nothing can beat that feeling of being on stage, and having an audience in the palm of your hand.

No matter how much I achieved, it was never enough. I always wanted more, and I think that's quite natural on a journey of growth where goals shift further away. Therefore, enjoying the journey along the way is just as important.

Celebrating your wins, both big and small, and being grateful for how far you've come is crucial and knowing that where you are you right now is exactly where you're supposed to be. More recently, I've learned to even be grateful for your pain too, and to pray from a place of gratitude rather than lack.

I'm immensely grateful for the opportunity to write music and perform with my best friends, people I love. I have the privilege of standing for something meaningful and important, using my voice and platform to champion the causes I believe in. Just because the cycle of The Tuts has come to an end for now, doesn't mean our roots aren't still there. I feared that people would forget about us. Yet, if I were more secure and self-validated we wouldn't have burned out, perhaps I would see my worth was more than just being productive and that it's okay to take a break. People will be fine with it, and I can always come back. Maybe we might never come back but that energy will transcend into my solo career in music in acting. Maybe when we least expect it we'll see a new bud appear on an old orchid. We just need to hibernate for a while and there can be nothing like nature to force you to take a break. Nature isn't always peace and harmony. It whispers to you but if you ignore the signs they get louder and louder.

Whilst working as a composer on a play, I had to attend a rehearsal on the other side of London. There happened to be severe weather warnings that day and advice was to not go outside but I ignored it, wanting to show up and prove that I was dedicated to the role, exemplifying a classic people-pleasing and scarcity mindset. I drove across London safely enough, but during rehearsal we heard a loud crashing noise outside. A massive tree had fallen directly on my car. I called my mum to break the news that the BMW One series she got me with her hard-earned working-class cash was now destroyed. Rightly so, she shouted and swore at me in all languages, English, Urdu,

Hindi. My white friends were shocked that my mum showed no concern or relief that I wasn't in the car when it was struck. They weren't used to brown mum rage but that's my mum's way of showing she cares. The car was written off and she got her money back but it was a stark reminder from mother nature that it will do what it wants and always has the final say. Just like punk, it doesn't conform, and you can't stop it from doing whatever the fuck it wants.

It's exhausting trying to keep balanced and be perfectly 'healed'. I sometimes even hate the concept of 'healing' as if to suggest I am broken in the first place. I am not broken. I don't need to be fixed. I'm okay just as I am. I'm just trying to survive in this capitalist world and use my gift of song writing to feel good about myself and play some shows to people who might relate.

Some of my coping mechanisms towards this apparent 'healing' are daily meditation, praying, reciting positive affirmations, journaling, walks, therapy, talking to friends, seeing my nieces, socialising with people I actually like who are uplifting and affirming, drinking celery juice (you will thank me when you have clear skin), cooking meals, having salt baths, talking to myself, making an effort to leave the house. There's also dining alone, solo dates, drowning negative thoughts with positive ones, not comparing one's self to anyone else. Open your heart and know that is okay to love others.

Nature taught me that, like the seasons, I can hibernate and rest. Nature doesn't feel ashamed of resting. It knows how to pause and reemerge in spring, shine in the summer, and, come autumn, let go like the leaves. If only we human beings followed this process with our own bodies.

When I am done resting, ready to reemerge like the spring daffodils, I won't let the music industry and capitalist living put me off. There's so much more I have to offer, and so much more

I want to accomplish. I've learned to trust the universe and believe that everything will happen in divine timing. All these things were meant to happen. I am still learning about self-love and worth and what it means. I'm getting better at regulating myself, but trauma never really goes away. It's always going to be there; we just gain tools to cope and manage it better until eventually, we grow bigger than it.

There's no rush to the top, slow and steady really does win the race, and longevity is the goal. At the same time, it's important to take action and show up for your dreams, to go against the grain and speak your truth. Nature showed me that it doesn't relent, the sun will rise and fall every day, and if you're not careful, it might destroy your car. Similarly, you don't have to wait for a label to sign you to release music or have an agent to be an actor, you can still do it without them. If I sat around waiting for someone to sign me, I'd have never released music.

Yes, I am Muslim and I am a punk, but that doesn't define me. Yes, I am someone who's experienced childhood trauma but that also doesn't define me. Song writing, acting, whatever it may be, is for me, a branch of nature co-creating with God. The truth lies in nature and punk is about speaking truths. Like nature, I am experiencing my death and my rebirth every day. If punk is nature and nature is God, I am punk by nature and that means God is punk!

Image description: black and white illustration of a fish with ornate embellishments on it and the waves around it.

The Gift of Healing

SUSMITA BHATTACHARYA

I received a special gift for my fortieth birthday – a diagnosis of breast cancer. Grade three invasive ductal carcinoma, to give it its proper terminology. I had been thinking of doing a challenge (sky diving had crossed my mind) but I'd never expected to go through such a massive challenge. This was, in a way, like sky-diving. Plummeting. Spiralling down towards an unknown destination. And I wasn't sure if I'd make it back to Earth alive.

There wasn't much time for reflection. Within two weeks of my diagnosis, I was booked in for my mastectomy, which would be followed by chemotherapy, radiotherapy and then ten years of taking an oestrogen receptive modulator. The first phase of the treatment plan would see me through autumn until spring of the following year. This was highly symbolic – how my darkest days were right in the middle of a bleak winter, and slowly, I would emerge on the other side of my treatment, to a new normal, a new life at the beginning of spring.

In her memoir, *The Undying*, poet Anne Boyer, writes that her doctor told her she could not avoid chemotherapy. If she did, it would be sure death. Her cancer was very aggressive, and her chemotherapy regimen was brutal. But it was something she could not avoid. For Boyer, the thought of submitting to the treatment would be like dying to be able to live. This was my case too, although my cancer was not aggressive, it still needed six cycles of chemotherapy and fourteen radiotherapy sessions, on top of the mastectomy, to hopefully clear any cancerous cells in my body. And to live, I'd have to go through some pretty rough side effects from all the drugs that would be blasted through my body over the next six months.

We were living in Devon at the time and the hospital was close to Dartmoor National Park, a place that has always been familiar to me, even while growing up in India, through reading books set in that backdrop. The tors and heather-covered landscape that came to life while through Daphne Du Maurier's and Charles Dickens' books had such a magnetic pull for me that it became a routine for my husband and I to complete the chemotherapy session, then drive down to the moors to catch the sunset, or look out for the wild ponies, to meditate and process what was happening to us. To stay still in the car and shed a few tears. To gather the strength to return home to two young children who would be quiet around me, knowing that their mother couldn't cope with too much noise and activity in the first couple of weeks of chemotherapy.

Those moments of quiet contemplation were so important for me, for us, to process the impact of the situation on our lives, to process the fear of what was lurking just around the corner, in the shadows, waiting to spring more unpleasant surprises on us. The landscape calmed our fears, and because my body had been heightened to feel with more intensity – new aches and pains, new fears, new reactions to the physical and emotional spheres of myself, the moors acted as a balm to soothe and prepare the body and mind for the hits and knocks that were to come.

I became acutely aware of the surroundings, changes in weather as my body changed due to the treatment. As my hair fell out, I felt the cold on my scalp and skin. My nose constantly leaked and my eyes watered. I began to feel grateful for the things we took for granted, or ignored the importance of. No nasal hair, no body hair, no eyelashes meant that regulating the temperature, keeping dust particles at bay were not possible at all. I felt the chill of the snow like never before, but it was also exhilarating to experience these new feelings and recognise the wonders of the human body and how it learns to cope with the most extremes of situations.

Being out in nature made me see things differently. I began to write poetry, using metaphor to explain my feelings, my way of processing the situation. I began to look for symbols, for meaning in the landscape around me. I noticed the relationship between mothers and their babies, the relationship between the sky and the birds, the water and the fish. Everything became more meaningful and clearer to me. A poem I wrote, 'Rivers', published in *Dust Poetry* magazine explored these feelings and symbolised how I was experiencing my illness at the time.

A river runs through my vein, courses red
and purple along the length of my arm,
takes with it the poison to destroy
the interloper who's found a home

in my breast. Three hours of feeding
my body this potion of drugs, I
stagger outdoors, suck in fresh air,
while this river burns inside,

stings, does its job. A river runs
through the moors, courses clear
and pure through the heather
padded land. White rapids

break the flow, a silver fish swims
downstream.
Cold mist envelops me, but I'm burning.
I scan the water, hoping the surge
will cool me down.

A river runs down
my eyes. I sit in this landscape and
wait for my body to fight back
or surrender.
Once the river in my vein has reached its
destination, and started its good work.
It is better I cry here, alone.
Prepare my smiles
and promises of tomorrow.

I watch
the birds fly back to their nests.
I hear them call to their young –
mothers
returning home.
Safe, for the night.

In her introduction to the poetry anthology, *The Poetry Cure*, Julia Darling says that poetry is a formidable influence, that can help people in their most difficult times and how finding the right allegory for suffering could help one feel in control of one's body and illness. Julia goes on to say that one of the hardest things about being unwell was feeling disabled and not in control of one's body. Writing poetry can make you feel in charge again. Waiting 'patiently' for an appointment can make one feel despondent and powerless, but writing poetry or doing something similarly engrossing would help to alleviate the worries to some extent. With her words offering solace, I sought to find more poetry in the natural world around me. Although the sea did offer me some peace, it was the moors that really held the key to my emotional stability. The changing of seasons could not be more dramatic there, and it was a stark visible reminder for me that time was passing, I was moving further along this journey, and there would be a day when all of this would end and a new chapter would begin.

Dartmoor was like a comfort blanket, wrapping me up in its warm, safe embrace. The familiarity with the moors was because of my childhood connection to the poem, 'The Highwayman', by Alfred Noyes. It was my absolute favourite poem, growing up, and the descriptions of the sky, the landscape, and the road all came to life when I sat in the car with my husband, observing the poem come to life in front of me.

> *The wind was a torrent of darkness among the gusty trees.*
> *The moon was a ghostly galleon tossed upon cloudy seas.*
> *The road was a ribbon of moonlight over the purple moor,*
> *And the highwayman came riding—*
> > *Riding—riding—*
> *The highwayman came riding, up to the old inn-door.*

This poem reminded me of the days when life was easy, without any problems. Always protected by my parents, who would ward off any harm that could befall me. Those memories washed over me once again, and despite my pain and worries, I'd feel safe and protected like a child again.

It is interesting to note how Virginia Woolf, in describing illness, used nature as an allegory to describe her symptoms and her pain. She compares ill health to unexplored countries, and how a bout of influenza is compared to wastelands and deserts; a fever resembles cliffs and abysses and gardens are filled with vivid flowers. For me too, the aftermath of each chemotherapy cycle was like being hit by a cyclone face-on. The speed at which the gale force winds came towards me, weakening my knees, making me fall to the ground and staying there, shaking like a rain battered tree, leafless, hairless, creaking and bending at breakpoint, hurting in the very core for two weeks, until the raging storm swept on, leaving behind an exhausted body, an exhausted mind, but not a broken soul. The soul, like the tree, curled up from its place on the ground, towards the sun, towards nourishment and hope. It drew strength and unfurled its branches again, embracing light and air, until the next storm hit, and then the next and then the next.

A couple of years after my treatment, I began to recuperate from the side effects of my treatment. I still lived inside a fog, unable to process my thoughts quickly or react to stimuli as swiftly as before. The medication post-treatment, Tamoxifen, a selective oestrogen receptive modulator, had its own issues and side effects to live with which I thought was even more difficult to accept than the primary treatment at the time of diagnosis. This was an ongoing ten-year treatment plan, which meant I'd have to experience continued brain fog, early onset menopause accompanied by hot flushes, joint pains, weight gain and anxiety. I just couldn't take off on long walks and spontaneous trips because of the anxiety, the fatigue and loss of self-confidence. I ended up worrying for days over train travel, something I had always done without even thinking about it. I lost sleep over going on family holidays – how would I cope on a day out, how could I go on long walks? These thoughts slowly ate into my enjoyment and quality of life. I became unsure about all the things I loved doing, especially travelling.

Two years after my treatment, we moved to another part of the country. It was going to be a new beginning for us in many ways, and although we welcomed this change, it was difficult to say goodbye to the place that had seen us through such tough times. It was hard to say goodbye to friends who stood by us, to our house that endured so much and brought us immense comfort. It was hard to say goodbye to the moors and the sea. I found every chance I could to return to Devon and meet up with friends. On one such trip, a couple of friends took me back to Dartmoor, and we spent a day walking along the River Dart. I paddled in the water while they swam, and we had a picnic lunch on the rocks by the riverbank.

This was a huge moment for me. I was able to walk for hours and did not feel exhausted. I lay down on the grass and closed my eyes, letting the sunshine warm me while I listened to the buzzing of the bees, the chirping of birds, the splash of the trout in the river, the bubbling of the water flowing past, the laughter of my friends splashing in the water, the smell of the wildflowers wafting by. I felt so alive. I was not worried about what was happening to me. I had submitted wholly and completely to nature, and in that moment, I felt her healing embrace.

I wrote a poem shortly after that magical experience, which marked my road to recovery in a holistic way. Although recovery is too simple a word to use, the process of healing is too complex. This was a significant moment when I thought I had overcome my greatest challenge, and I began to look forward, rather than backwards. Writing this poem brought me full circle to where I had started on my cancer journey. Being published in a journal dedicated to Dartmoor couldn't have been a better place for it.

THE TROUT

The trout knows her destination — flexing
upstream, her rainbow scales glinting

in the rush of sun-dappled spray. She shoots
through the Dart like a life-giving drug. The
river — an intravenous cannula which injects the
promise of health.
If I stand silent on this moss-softened bank
I can hear my breath whispering,
my heart pounding to the beat of the
woodpecker's tattoo.
The trees close in on me like a mother's embrace,
the skeins of spiderweb caressing my face.
I close my eyes, lose myself to all
this restoration.
The shingle path leads me ahead.
I take another step forward and
I become that trout —
A medley of colour, muscling my way up
against the current.

Ten years after my diagnosis, life has changed in many ways, and
I don't want the positives to be overshadowed by the negatives.
The two gifts I received since this life-changing illness, is that
I have come to appreciate nature and poetry a lot more. I am
thankful for all the positivity they bring into my life, for the
strength I have gained by writing poems, and for the awareness
I now have in enjoying the gifts nature brings to my doorstep.
Very special gifts indeed.

Image description: black and white illustration of numerous tree trunks entwined to seemingly make a single tree.

The Sacred Arbor

Trees, Mythology and Islamic Perspectives

HANAN ISSA

I n Islamic history, there's a story about a crying tree. The Prophet Muhammad used to give sermons while leaning against the trunk of a date palm tree until a more formal prayer space was built and a pulpit placed in the mosque. It was said that people heard a painful wailing sound and traced it back to the tree trunk. The Prophet held the tree until it stopped crying and explained that the tree missed him and his followers' company. A sweet story that highlights the Prophet Muhammad's gentle nature as well as a potential origin for the term 'treehugger'? Though, when I first heard this story, all I could think of was: 'What does a crying tree sound like?'

There are lots of stories about trees in Islamic literature – from gargantuan trees once worshipped as gods, to the tree still standing in Syria today that is believed to have once given shade to the Prophet Muhammad as a child. The most significant tree in Islamic teachings has a name: Sidratul Muntaha. Sidr is a type of lote tree mostly known for the honey that bees make from its flowers. Highly sought after for its antioxidant properties, Sidr honey can sell for over £300 a kilo. Muntaha is an Arabic word, most commonly used today as a woman's name, that means 'utmost'. Sidratul Muntaha, the utmost lote tree, sits at the boundary of all known worlds. It is the last known entity between everything in existence and the realm that only Allah inhabits.

I've googled lote trees. There's nothing spectacular about their appearance. They are shaped how most people would line-draw a tree with leaves. As I write this, I'm wondering if the lote tree looks so generic because it looks like every simple drawing of a tree or if these simple drawings came from the first person trying to draw a lote tree. Either way, the image of a lote tree seems to be firmly rooted, pardon the pun, in our collective consciousness.

But it's this humbly-shaped tree that exists at the cross-roads between the heavens and the earth where, it is said, even the knowledge of the angels stops. A guardian between what is known and what is not. I'm reminded of the Tree of Knowledge in the Bible. It doesn't exist in the Qur'anic version of Adam and Eve's disobedience. In Islam, the tree isn't specifically called anything except by Satan who describes it to Adam as the Tree of Immortality/Everlasting Life and it is this, the concept of eternal life, with which he tempts Adam. It's an interesting divergence, immortality instead of knowledge is the 'forbidden fruit' for humankind. I think back over the history of Islam, from the very first word of Allah revealed to the Prophet Muhammad being 'read' to Al-Qarawiyyin, the world's first university, established in 857 by Fatima al Fihri in Morocco – learning and gaining knowledge has always been a core part of the faith: An achievable, attainable, noble quest. Perhaps that is why the more abstract and impossible goal of immortality was presented as the 'forbidden fruit'?

It's something I think about a lot. Early on in our marriage, my husband and I used to hike in the Bannau Brecheiniog, most weekends. We would often collapse halfway under a tree somewhere and fall asleep, faces shaded by what Kahlil Gibran once described as 'poems the earth writes upon the sky'. I'm not sure if walking through woods and fields to the point of exhaustion, and then falling asleep under the shade of a tree changed us. I'd like to think we thanked the tree for what it provided but I don't remember. And you can find folklore and customs that range the spectrum of opinions on trees and rest. In certain Indian traditions it is considered unsafe to sleep under certain types of trees, the Peepal for example, as that, it is believed, is where vengeful ghosts like to hang about. Alternatively, part of some Aboriginal death rituals is to wrap the remains of the dead and leave them in the fork of a tree to rest.

In Qur'anic metaphor, trees are sometimes used to explain the concept of truth:

أَلَمْ تَرَ كَيْفَ ضَرَبَ ٱللَّهُ مَثَلًا كَلِمَةً طَيِّبَةً كَشَجَرَةٍ طَيِّبَةٍ أَصْلُهَا ثَابِتٌ وَفَرْعُهَا فِى ٱلسَّمَآءِ ٢٤

Do you not see how Allah compares a good word to a good tree? Its root is firm and its branches reach the sky,

تُؤْتِىٓ أُكُلَهَا كُلَّ حِينٍۭ بِإِذْنِ رَبِّهَا ۗ وَيَضْرِبُ ٱللَّهُ ٱلْأَمْثَالَ لِلنَّاسِ لَعَلَّهُمْ يَتَذَكَّرُونَ ٢٥

῾always῾ yielding its fruit in every season by the Will of its Lord. This is how Allah sets forth parables for the people, so perhaps they will be mindful.

This tie between trees and spirituality is present in almost every faith on the planet. The motif of the Tree of Life isn't just a symbol of man's arrogance and downfall. Their strength, longevity and flexibility have inspired people throughout time to connect with the intangible – the unknown, spiritual, soul. Any time I sit under splayed branches for shade or hear the susurration whispering through leaves I am reminded of the centuries this tree has witnessed. An almost immortal guardian with which we live in an eternal cycle of reciprocation: its oxygen for our CO_2, over and over again. In recent years, science has revealed that even traces of our DNA have been found within the trunks of trees. Similar to the ancient Mayan belief that the Yaxche tree was a channel through which souls would travel between worlds, whereas Yggdrasil in Norse mythology is the great tree on which Odin hanged himself in order to see into the underworld and gain knowledge of the runes:

> *Then I was fertilized and became wise;*
> *I truly grew and thrived.*
> *From a word to a word I was led to a word,*
> *From a work to a work I was led to a work.*

This extract, taken from the anonymous text *The Poetic Edda*, speaks of being led from word to word, work to work; an albeit abstract journey from one space to another, from ignorance to knowledge. And yet again we see a tree located right on the boundary between.

I remember starting my period while climbing a tree. As my scraped arms reached for the next branch, I felt a thick wetness through my shorts. Soon after I was staring down into the toilet bowl watching red lines, like smoke, dance through the water. My transition from one world to another – childhood to womanhood – and all the baggage that would soon come with it stained me like the dark red patch I had left on the tree. And for me, it was a pivotal moment crossing from not knowing and knowing. I hadn't had much of a heads-up about periods and my initial thought was that I was dying. It wasn't until after I had gone inside and plucked up the courage to talk to my mum that she explained how normal this was. All part of growing up and 'becoming a woman'. And that battling this pain and discomfort would, unfortunately, be a part of my life going forward.

The idea of trees as crossroads between worlds and wisdom, knowing and unknowing is so infused in our history and culture that it has even permeated our folklore. In the Book of Taliesin, there are fragments of poems known as 'Cad Goddeu' (The Battle of the Trees). This text, believed by some to contain hidden Druidic rituals, tells the story of a battle between the magician Gwydion and Arawn, King of Annwn:

Rithwch riedawc wyd.
Gantaw yn lluyd.
A rwystraw peblic.
Kat arllaw annefic.
Pan swynhwyt godeu.
Y gobeith an godeu.

'Conjure up majestic trees',
'in great numbers
and resist the mob'.
When trees were conjured up,
there came a mighty, bounteous host:
hope itself approached.

The long poem goes on to list the many varieties of trees fighting in the battle that include alder, willow, rowan, cherry, blackthorn, almond, pine, hazel, beech, gorse and many others. As a hardcore Tolkien fan, it's hard not to picture the Ents' assault on Isengard, fighting the corrupted wizard Saruman in his attempt to scourge Middle Earth. Though, in all honesty, the idea of trees, guardians and crossroads infused with wisdom and warmth, fighting in any battle feels just as jarring as imagining the sound of a tree crying.

Trees have come to fit a very specific aesthetic, particularly within the modern wellness industry. Now they are sanctuaries of peace, woodland is a space to recharge and relax. Guided meditations talk you through a forest walk in a bid to destress and take a break from day-to-day worries. But what if your work is in the forest? A friend told me she knew a forestry worker that gave up on guided meditations since they often asked listeners to imagine a woodland to relax but all she saw was work. Much like most urbanites might struggle to find peace picturing a grey-carpeted office. During lockdown my husband, son and I would pile into the car driving the allowed amount of miles from our home to a nearby stretch of woodland. My son hunted for goblins masquerading as stumps while my husband found his favourite hollow tree, peering out from between the cracked bark. I liked looking up at the canopy. I'm reminded of how similar the curved stretches of tall trees are to the architecture of a cathedral. Both spaces invite spiritual reflection, full of hopeful susurrant prayers for a future where all the love and sacrifice shown to us is appreciated and returned.

But universality is tricky. It's hard to homogenise anything, even trees, knowing how varied the world's interpretations are for their presence. Is it a tree of knowledge or immortality that tempts the most? Are trees symbols of rest or work? Will sleeping beneath the boughs of an oak provide a sense of eternal peace or encourage vengeful spirits to haunt us?

One thing we do know is that trees do an awful lot of work for us. They provide us with the air we breathe or are chopped down and used to make other essentials such as paper. Shel Silverstein's *The Giving Tree* exemplifies this somewhat unreciprocated relationship perfectly. The boy takes from his love, a tree, first its fruit, then its branches until all that remains is a stump. Often viewed as a tale of love and generosity, the book's author suggested a much darker inspiration: of extreme self-sacrifice. The tree is willing to give everything of herself to make the boy happy, who blithely continues to take and take and take without a care for the consequences.

I'm wondering if this is a reality. Are we still forcing trees to give everything for almost nothing in return? It is surprisingly difficult to get any definitive stats on deforestation in 2023 but according to the World Wildlife Foundation, there was a 60% drop in deforestation in the Amazon from January 2022 to January 2023. I'm not convinced this suggests a greater sense of care for the world's forests but I'm quietly hopeful this points to, at least, a slow shift away from us re-enacting Silverstein's boy character simply taking and taking and taking.

The importance of caring for the environment is so intrinsically part of the Islamic faith that Muslims are encouraged to plant seeds even if the world itself is ending. Islam gives all human beings the title of 'Khalifah' or steward over this earth. Often contextualised into meaning some sort of dictatorial leader, like most Arabic words it has another interpretation – that of caretaker. Some verses refer specifically to the earth's rights over us as its inhabitants, one being that, even in times of warfare, no trees should be cut down as a result. Another verse describes 'the servants of the Most Compassionate [as those who] walk gently/humbly on this earth'. I only felt truly connected to this verse very recently. Eid prayers during the summer months are held in a local park when the weather is good. Hundreds, if not thousands, of Muslim families come decked out in their most beautiful clothes, ready to spread greetings of Salam and many, many sweets. This year, I drove past an hour or so afterwards and the field was completely empty. No littering from the sweets or uprooted patches of grass left from the bouncy castle. No evidence at all of this huge gathering remained. We had tread softly on this patch of earth.

I am, unashamedly, biased when I say that this is faith at its most nourishing, when based on a sense of care – for self, for others, for the landscape, for the future. Dod yn ôl at fy nghoed is a Welsh phrase commonly used to mean a healthy mindset or coming back to one's senses. Interestingly, the literal translation is 'to return to my trees'. Trees as bringers of sense, of balance, of wisdom, of transition, of life. Every day discoveries are made providing more and more insight into how trees care for one another, the spaces around them, and how they communicate and even speak. Our relationship with these ancient beings continues to shift over time. Here's hoping the next phase will emerge as reciprocal, rooted in care and curiosity, not crying.

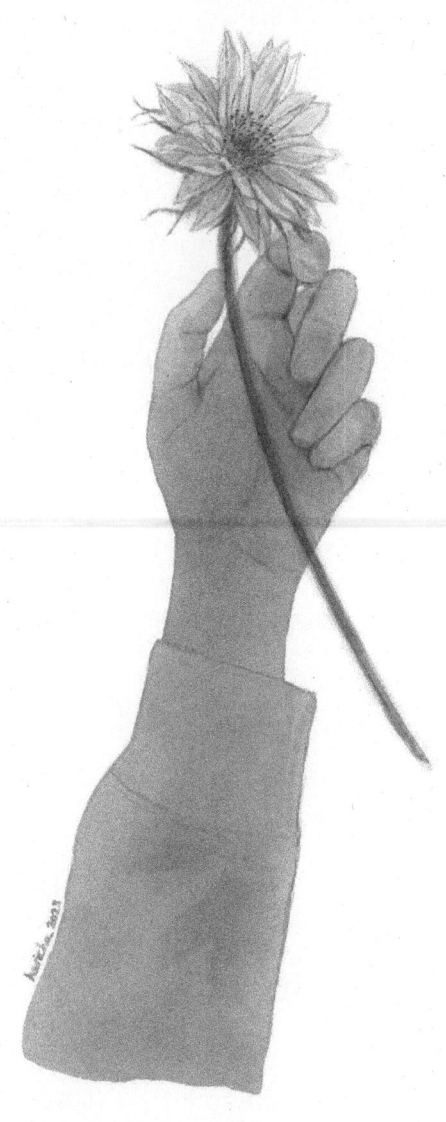

Image description: black and white illustration of a hand in a long-sleeved top, holding a flower.

an ecostory

KHAIRANI BAROKKA

i.

below is a space
containing a tenet of
indigenous minang cosmology.

one of thousands
of indigenous cosmologies,
from an archipelago of more than 17,000 islands,

for relating to the earth.

also within these two brackets:
the refusal for it to be translated.

we are beset
by constant socioecological crises,
demanding indigenous and peasant land
be destroyed for 'development'

—mines-dams-plantations-factories-malls-tunnels-military-
bases-militarytestsites-touristtraps-cities—

destroying ecologies,
of which indigenous populations
are protectors.

anything translated into english,
or even written in any language
within exposed environs, risks capture.

is capture.

is shareable, and thus liable
to be owned by a corporate entity.

the same corporations who have,
from the time of the dutch east india company—
that state-owned proto-megacorp—
used any sharing in good faith,
or under coercion,
of indigenous knowledge
to murder,
poison, bribe, maim, and,
ultimately,
evict caretakers of the earth
from that earth.

[   ]

ii.

during the ecoliterature panel, the white woman in the
middle says 'of course, all this was done to make people's
lives better.'

connected by a shimmer of invisible string, the caribbean
writer on her other side and i say, in succession:

that we have come from islands wrecked and robbed by
forced industrial revolution. for blood and for plunder.
earths clutched, imperial fists.

the woman in the middle ignores us. an award-winning
'nature writer', she proclaims she is more worried about
brexit than climate change. look at china, she says, and their
great policies. governments are doing the work. everyone
should just move to the cities, she says, leave 'nature' be.

we flank her on the stage;
yet i can hear our voices in the microphones
drowned in her ears,
and in the ears of those in the audience
who hear only her voice.

what i need to remember,
with more clarity, and grace:

the instant thread
between two island writers,
indies west and east,
who refused to leave before speaking. who refused to ever
be drowned.

here is that thread, so i do not lose it:

[   ]

iii. every instance of people using 'anthropocene' to mean only the last hundred years feels like sandpaper on the skin.

this is the definition myself and many kin have clung to, even before i read these words:

> 'the Anthropocene is not a new event, but is rather the continuation of practices of dispossession and genocide, coupled with a literal transformation of the environment, that have been at work for the last five hundred years. Further, the Anthropocene continues a logic of the universal which is structured to sever the relations between mind, body, and land.'
>
> – heather david and zoe todd

i imagine a world in which all uses of anthropocene use this definition.

that world is here:

[   ]

iv. at a reading, m. nourbese phillip quotes yoruba philosopher bayo akomolafe, and resonance hits my whole body—as it does every time I reread this quote:

> 'What we rudely call "nature" today does not even have a name in Yoruba culture because there was no distinction between us and the goings-on around us,' Akomolafe says. The Yoruba religion of Ifa, he explains, sees a 'vitality' in the nonhuman world.
>
> 'Mountains could be consulted, trees could have privileges,' he adds.'

the resonance:
the understanding that this is my philosophy as well
our communal philosophies in our archipelago
thousands of them
echo this quote

the resonance:
that not only people who are recognised as professional
philosophers know what akomolafe said to be true
that children with links of indigeneity are taught this
carry this knowledge within our whole bodies
to be remembered our whole lives

the body feeling illuminated
as it is reminded

and the opposite:
this is the rub, here—
what do you mean by 'nature'
if you don't want to give land back

v.

'you' just above
refers to colonial settlers
not only in the us
canada
new zealand
australia
indonesia, as coloniser of papua

but their tentacles in the corporate land grabs
ferociously devouring our islands

until their idea of paradise:
our oblivion

in an alternate reality
a multiverse
none of this extractivism takes place
reversal not even required
as it never happened

and the seas exhale in relief:

[   ]

vi. every national park in settler colonial states is illegally declared. is built on mass eviction of those who lived in greatest harmony with the flows of life in those lands.

this is true in colonial histories of eco-assault, against pluriversal african indigenous communities

and in what is now known as the americas, as latin america. as australasia. as virtually, increasingly, every soil and sea.

the contemporary version of this behavior increasing: 'biodiversity credits'. 'carbon offsetting'. ways to buy land off indigenous inhabitants. ways to numerically pin a tombstone to strands of life.

vii. triage.

more than a decade ago, i come up to the illustrious asian-american artist after her talk, about her project with regards to purchasing land off indigenous peoples for 'carbon offsetting'. i try to tell her, and am brushed off, as has happened before when i am (perceived to be) less powerful than the one brushing off.

we argue as she says 'we need triage'. for her, rainforests are numbers, so removed from the taking of indigenous lives. so removed from how enumerating life begets the actual delay of climate action—that real climate action, real triage work, would be returning land to indigenous peoples, and making sure we keep them, instead of turning rainforest into managed properties by the arrogance of technocrats.

that her actions are accelerating climate change.
that indigenous peoples are the best caretakers of rainforest—a recognised fact that management consultants run circus-circles around us to minimise.

viii. the artist s. sudjojono (1913-1986) teaches us
that the dutch cultivated war through oil on canvas—
teaches us the concept:

mooi indie.

beautiful indies.

'landscape art' and vistas of indonesian beauty, glossing over hundreds of years of brutally violent genocides, slavery, and extractivism.

this is paradise, the canvases teach outsiders, and try to inculcate in ourselves.

this land is for your taking, their canvasses teach europe,

teach colonial settlers.

decades on, bali is choked by waves of expanding beer bottles, drunk aussies, eat-pray-love antivaxxer families flocking to ubud.

'that's why we came to bali, to heal', says the australian woman in my poetry workshop (which, as per the insistence of my friends and i to the australian literary festival organisers, would be half-populated by native balinese women, not just tourists).

she does not see the balinese women in the room.

she does not see me.

she does not see the mass graves from 1965-'66 in balinese soil, a genocide that literally killed off what was, until then, the world's largest feminist movement. an 'anti-leftist' genocide. cold war casualties. american arms. american hit lists that spread, unbearably.

she does not see the earth she walks on.

ix. a european journalist is connected to me via a curator. he is writing about biodiversity.

in our discussion, i mention the devastating 2015 forest fires in indonesia.

he admits he'd covered them, that he was there, but chose to write only of orangutan extinction threat. that he had omitted 'the social justice angle', erroneously.

nearly 100,000 people died in those fires.

it was not seen as a genocide. the 'social justice angle' was not then apparent.

even my journalism work seems extractive, he says.

yes, i think, as i realise what i have not gained from the day.

yes, i think, as i wonder whether he knows 'orang utan' means person, or people, of the forest in indonesian. that we regard them as forest people, just like us, that we want their survival as much as ours, our fates interlinked—but unlike us, they are seen through much different lenses, recorded differently.

x. i watch gargantuan student protests in jakarta from a screen. my brother is on the health and safety team, carries a body to safety. the tear gas spreads and spreads. when they tear gas the clinic—the clinic—i weep.

the students had many demands. repeated these often. among them, an end to the tragically now-passed omnibus law, enabling even more environmental extractivism. among them, an appeal for better laws that protect sexual assault victims, that ensure sex outside wedlock is not criminalised.

in australia, these mass protests are reported on as being against a 'sex law'.

indonesians protest until their coverage more accurately reflects reality.
these were environmental protests too, for one.

how easily, how comically the australian press confirms their obsession with smashing in bali, how that is all we are to them—a place to be sexually free on a beach.

mooi, mooi indie.

at a later date, an australian woman engages in an ill-advised online argument with me.

'where are the indonesian environmental protests? i've never heard of them.' is the exact argument.

xi. technological surveillance of
environmental activist homes,
from one nation-state to the next,
brazil to indonesia,
means invasion in the form of anxiety.

here is a true story i would like to tell you about surveillance:

[   ]

here, another:

[   ]

here is one from january 2022:

[   ]

i am trying to learn
from the quietest.

to quieten my anxiety.

(lifelong fear of saying too much
from dictatorship childhood
to present microphone danger.)

their thoughts and words and ideas
are stolen from,
unattributed.
they do not care
if it helps protect lands
and those lands' peoples

(though i care
about their names,
and it chafes).

they are off the grid

or try to be

or are public in a way
that they hope
will not assassinate them,
as their friends have suffered.

many continue to sacrifice
notoriety and wealth
for ecological succour,
indigenous continuance.

my teachers have always
spoken to me in brackets:

[   ]

i honour them
by keeping secrets.

this will always be an ecostory.

the spaces between these brackets
are an opening
doorway
entrance to a universe.

they lead to the same place,
to places that contain each other.

different biomes communicating,
maintaining themselves,
they hold and hold each other.

this is how the warming earth
can keep itself:
the spaces we hold for refusal,
the echoes of persistent undercurrents.

marronage of the persecuted living,
human and otherwise.
a fugitive earth,
a beating pulse.

the only way i can bring myself to write it:

[   ]

References

'Nigeria's Bayo Akomolafe: We aren't 'in control' of climate crisis'. *Deutsche Welle* Online. Last accessed April 20, 2022. dw.com/en/nigerias-bayo-akomolafe-we-arent-in-control-of-climate-crisis/a-54081002.

Davis, H. and Todd, Z., 2017. On the Importance of a Date, or Decolonizing the Anthropocene, *ACME: An International Journal for Critical Geographies*, *16*(4), pp.761-780.

harcha 2023

Image description: black and white illustration of two figures facing the sea's horizon at a shore edge. One of the figures has their arms spread out.

Until We Turn the Tide

TINA PASOTRA

There is a picture of me standing next to my sister, I'm maybe four or five years old. I'm wearing a blue swimming costume, arms outstretched, and echoing the expanse of the sea behind me. If my memory serves me right, this was the first time I went to the beach with my mum. Manorbier Beach, in Pembrokeshire, Wales. Although my memories are fractured, I do recall a mermaid's tail made out of wet sand that my mum artfully molded to cover my hairy little legs. I remember the smell of the coast. Seaweed and salt. Smells unique to the place that I recognise as home.

When I was asked to contribute towards this collection of thoughts around our connection to nature, my first thought was, obviously, my love for the sea. I mean, my Instagram mainly consists of images and videos of my visits to the coast and my year-round sea swimming. My favourite jacket is embroidered with Bruce Lee's wisdom — 'Be water, my friend'. Even my astrological birth chart (Cancer Sun, Scorpio Moon) is a double water sign. Before I started to write this piece, I worried I had not read enough to warrant pen to paper. How would I describe the language of the body in words? Something so visceral, that can only really be felt.

Now, before I bang on about my love of the sea, I'd like to

share some of my backstory. Back in the '80s, when my mum was pregnant with me, and my sister was eighteen months old. She lived with her sister, brother in law and their two-year-old son. Cramped in an overcrowded high-rise flat in Luton – an inhospitable environment with no access to outdoor space or nature. It took time for her to fight for a council house so that we would have 'better' living conditions and a proper house with a garden. When she did manage to secure a new house, she planted an apple tree in the garden. A symbol of the right to have a space in which she could grow and cultivate and make her own. Unfortunately, my mum never witnessed the growth of that tree. That was because she made the courageous decision to run away from the forced marriage she was in at the time. I can't comprehend the gravity of her decision. That she had to leave behind her entire community and the people she loved. I often feel like she left a part of herself behind, planted in that unforgotten tree.

Many years later, in 2018, as an adult, I visited Punjab, India and my extended family for the first time. I am a multi-disciplinary artist, and my work is an ongoing exploration into the ways our body expresses, carries, and transforms our lived experience. I'm interested in work that draws attention to the complex relationships of our bodies to domestic and natural environments, family, and the nexus of past, present and future modalities of time. My work also engages with identity, the dynamics of power and moments to pursue pleasure and rest. I had secured arts funding from the British Council for a research project. This project was linked to my research on the Partition of India, which forced millions of people to leave their homes (including my family) due to the violence of British colonial rule 'ending' in 1947. Obviously, this was something I was never taught in school or discussed with family. The trip was also connected to the development of *I CHOOSE* – my short film based on my mum's experiences and the experiences of other women like her. Therefore my visit was multilayered and interconnected through a creative, artistic, research, and personal lens. On reflection, I don't think I was mentally prepared for the emotional overwhelm I would feel upon meeting my extended family for the first time. Not being able to speak enough Punjabi, and all the untethered emotions that came from not growing up with my Sikh community.

Upon landing in Punjab, we drove to my family's farm. They harvest wheat and rice. The landscape was completely flat. This was a very different perspective from what I was used to with the dramatic landscape of Wales, with its rolling mountains and the rugged coast. As we drove into the farm, I noticed a bush of wild roses growing by one of the walls. In that moment feeling homesick for Wales, I found comfort in watching them dance in the breeze. The sun was strikingly orange, perfectly round, and felt almost close enough to touch. It was the first time my feet had tread on this land. I was both a stranger and familiar to the family I had met for the first time. How could I not feel connected to my family lineage and its ongoing relationship with the land? The food I ate came from their hands and the fields that I had just walked on. I felt embarrassed to have such little knowledge of growing food and how soil rarely passes through my fingertips. But I reminded myself that shame is not helpful, and that learning is not an endpoint. It remains a journey of learning and unlearning. Instead, I thought of how this attachment to the land has been passed down to me, from my Punjab all the way to Wales. Whilst I do not want to romanticise the arduous labour of my family and the land they inhabit, I know that it is a fundamental part of my identity. There was a reason that my mum chose Wales to run away to, having been inspired by the landscape itself on a passing journey, many years before. It is this tracing of my family and my mum's relationship to the land that makes me grateful to be connected to the landscape of Wales and my access to the mountains, and the sea.

Although I have always had a love for the sea, there were poignant moments where this love and respect were deepened. In my twenties, I experienced a severe episode of depression. For those who haven't been through it, depression is a selfish illness that robs you and your loved ones of time and joy. The most basic of tasks became mammoth, and pleasure inconsequential. I was deeply fortunate to be cared for by those who might not be considered conventional caregivers by the standards of nuclear family ideals. It was these loved ones who dragged me out to the coast as an act of care for me – practising an extension of care that moved beyond their 'own'. Something that I think is often echoed within nature's ecosystems, like how dolphins travel in pods, groups of hundreds and thousands, welcoming other species to swim and eat together. Trees communicate their needs and 'talk' with one another, sending nutrients via a network of fungi buried in the soil. Reminding us that care is a collective endeavour.

In those moments, even though I felt no connection to anything, I was still being nourished by the sea. Something I would come to realise later on. I like to think that with those moments void of feeling, the land holds you even when you are unable to hold yourself. I find it comforting to appreciate how insignificant we are in comparison to the vastness of nature. I find myself holding back on describing what nature feels like in fear of the 'cliché', but as the saying goes, 'Clichés are clichés because they are true'. Nature is the one place where I feel an immediate sense of presence and belonging.

In October 2019, a friend of mine encouraged me to embrace sea swimming during the winter. Until this point, when I said I love the sea, I meant sitting on the beach or bathing my body in water during the summer months. This did not include November to March. So when my friend suggested we go swimming in freezing cold water, I thought *Jog on, babes*. Still, there was always going to be a part of me that was up for a challenge, so I gave it a shot. I expected the water to be icy cold, but it was still relatively warm. The practice of Pranayama eased me into it. Pranayama is the fourth of the Eight Limbs of Yoga, commonly understood as breathwork. I'm by no means an expert on this practice of breath, however, I want to honour this use of breath given the endless co-option of ancestral techniques not receiving its due respect. It was this that helped me regulate my body and my senses every time I stepped into the water, and even now when the nerves kick in.

Fast forward to 2023, a bobble hat, wetsuit gloves and socks. The sky is blue, the air crisp and we look up. The snow falls, gently kissing the tip of my nose. I take a deep breath. No matter how many times I've gotten in the sea in winter, I still get nervous because I know it will be freezing! Pranayama helps me navigate that. After that initial swim in October 2019, I went back every month, and now I've been in the sea throughout every season. I'm familiar with its rhythms and how it changes through spring, summer, autumn and winter. Now my loved ones notice if it has been a bit too long, and ask 'When were you last in the sea?' I think it's a subtle cue when my mood is off and they have received both 'Tina before and after the sea'. It feels like a deep reset and a literal purge. Checking the forecast for full sun the night before, travelling down in the dark mornings, timing my entry into the sea, to rise with the sun is hands down one of my favourite things to do. In those moments, I'm hoping I can hold onto the gratitude felt and carry this back to land, into everyday life.

There are different schools of thought and research on cold-water swimming. I only speak from what I feel my experiences have been. Some research suggests that the stress of the cold activates the fight or flight response. How we adapt has the potential to make us less reactive to the shock, and in turn, could also make us less reactive to the stressors of daily life. This is something I have felt. Now I notice my much more grounded approach when confronted with stress in my own life. Now, this isn't a cute advert for cold water immersion, and I know there's a difference between an ice bath in the garden versus having the gift of the coast on your doorstep – but I do want to emphasise that the impact on my mental health has been really significant. I have bathed my body all over Wales, from South to West and North. I find it difficult to pick my favourite swim spot because they all hold a beauty that's unique to that place. I also make a conscious decision to wear a bikini instead of a wetsuit, even in the winter, because I want my body to be closely connected to the water. Whenever possible, I swim naked, too. There's always a nervous exhale, my breath deepens and then I submerge. It's calm despite being bitterly cold but you're in and forced into nothing but that moment.

Growing up in environments where nature is immediately present inevitably shapes how we see the world. My creativity is always in conversation with nature and I feel forever indebted to its gift. Beyond the sea's lessons, I'm mesmerised by its infinite knowledge – knowing we probably haven't even scratched the bottom of its wonder.

As I finish this essay, it's nearly time for me to attend my first international artist residency in Oaxaca and my feelings are naturally a mix of excitement and nerves. I was drawn to this particular place due to its relationship with land and people. I wonder who I will meet, and what lessons or dreams will be conjured when listening to the Pacific's voice – the first time I will swim in this ocean. Having the opportunity to experience a new landscape and swim in the Pacific for the first time is a privilege I cherish. I didn't grow up travelling the world and so embarking on these adventures as an adult fills me with a youthful wonder and curiosity.

As I plan my trip, I go back to that picture of me standing next to my sister. I go back to my mum planting that tree. Land and sea punctuate significant moments in my life and the common theme of nature is the one holding us. I'm reminded in times of feeling lonely, we're never too far from belonging as nature shows me, time and time again.

Image description: black and white illustration of the Napo moist tropical forest river with three row boats sailing down it into the distance.

The Nature of White Sustainability

SHARAN DHALIWAL

Sustainability's recent growth resides within white ideals. By that I mean, the unhealthy consumption of the land we live on, has led to the need for significant change within a capitalist system. If we accept that 'white ideals' sit within consumption through capitalism, we can see that while living off natural resources is inevitable for our species to survive, there are two ways of doing it: violently or gently. An influx in consumerism has caused a more violent approach over the years – with a growing population, the capitalist agenda grew alongside it in order to fulfil the needs of the mass populace. We wanted to own more and with an ever-changing world, we wanted to own every new development of these products. This was sold to us as the only way to survive the complex institutions that were erected to encourage economic growth. Because of this economic growth, those in power got richer and greedier. While we continue to participate in that system, we have very little choice on how to survive otherwise.

Now, I asked you to accept 'white ideals' as consumption through capitalism but didn't give you the space to consider that. What I'm talking about is how capitalism comes hand in hand with white supremacy: as the Global North dominated industry growth in the early 1900s, it used Black, minority ethnic and Indigenous labour to achieve this. Not just labour but also land, produce and natural resources. Capitalism effectively destroys a land that was originally used to consume in a (more or less) gentle way. For example, the most biodiverse place on Earth is Yasuni, located inside the Napo moist tropical forest in north-eastern Ecuador, which is part of the Amazonian rainforest. It has a few different tribes of Indigenous folk living there, maintaining the environmental balance of the thousands of species that reside inside of it. The Napo moist tropical forest in north-eastern Ecuador has about 600 species of birds, 200 species of mammals, 500 species of fish, and 150 species of frogs in the park[1]. This land lives peacefully with the people who move within it, according to what the land needs. We know that this is how Indigenous folks lived before they were colonised, and so we can deduce that Indigenous lifestyles are the most sustainable and beneficial. According to the 2018 National Geographic, there are around 370 million Indigenous people living on roughly 24% of the world. They are the communities which protect 80% of the world's biodiversity.

I'm not saying all white people have these ideals, or that every white person is a supremacist. When I say 'white', I'm talking about power systems created on the back of colonialism and imperialism. The inherent driving force is the concept of 'whiteness' which goes beyond skin colour.

What I've noticed in the recent trend in white sustainability, is how it rides on the coattails of Indigenous people's livelihoods – from how they exist, eat, produce. But when Indigenous

1   "Indigenous peoples defend Earth's biodiversity—but they're in danger", Gleb Raygorodetsky. *National Geographic*, 16 November 2018. nationalgeographic.com/environment/article/can-indigenous-land-stewardship-protect-biodiversity-

people are introduced to the conversation, the uncomfortable truth is revealed: racism is deep rooted in environmentalism. This does a few things: it ignores those at the frontlines of harm, it continues theft, and it forwards the rhetoric of white saviourism. Because if whiteness, in other words capitalism, had a big hand in creating this climate crisis, then when saving the land, should they not turn to those who consumed gently to become the leaders of change?

It seems they have instead taken Indigenous practises and made them their own. From rubbing turmeric all over yourselves and deciding to sell it in fancy packaging to Debra down the street, who has vague ideas of India being in a continent with the other browns. To veganism centring whiteness, when the ethical and plant-based way of life has historically sat within many Asian and African cultures.

In fact, those practises have now been introduced into the capitalist model – sustainability is a growing industry, and while it helps reduce our carbon footprint, we need to be cautious with what we believe. The Competition and Markets Authority (CMA) states that the consumer protection law 'does not prevent businesses from making environmental claims about their products and services, provided they do not mislead consumers. It provides a framework for businesses to make environmental claims that help consumers make informed choices. Consumer protection law therefore gives consumers important protection in relation to environmental claims'.[2] It is considered as unlawful to claim something is eco or sustainable without backing it up with evidence – and the CMA may take you to court if these regulations aren't met sufficiently.

---

2 "Making environmental claims on goods and services" Competition & Markets Authority, *gov.uk*. gov.uk/government/publications/green-claims-code-making-environmental-claims/environmental-claims-on-goods-and-services#fn:1

It isn't just about the food itself, but the packaging, the transportation, wages and labour. We can't assume a company's ethics based on any labels they own because we don't know the history of where the products are from and the eco footprint of anything beyond the product itself. Is it sustainable to farm the volume of food we currently are, which could very well be harming agriculture? Are we pushing agriculture to produce more than it naturally does? Gentle consumption involves listening to the land, the animals, bacteria, and being patient. But with a large population, and so many needs wanting to be met, the way in which we produce hurts the land. We devour more of it and cause more environmental damage.

The effect it then has on the working communities in this production, is often overlooked. As we demand more, we are asking from the manual and emotional labour from communities of colour. If whiteness is represented through a concrete jungle, communities of colours as labourers, are working in a green oasis.

The UK's Food Standards Agency Chief Scientist, Robin May, stated in a 2021 blog post: 'At present, there are no internationally agreed standards for environmental sustainability labelling and no agreement on what "sustainable production" should measure: carbon dioxide release, water use, biodiversity impact? Consequently, there is no easy way for consumers to make evidence-based purchasing decisions about the environmental impact of their diet.' He goes on to say, 'transforming the food system into one that is fully sustainable relies on a central premise – that the environmental footprint of foods is known'[3] and I would add: how the food is produced. Not just

---

3 "The urgency of eco-labelling in light of COP26."
Professor Robin May, *gov.uk*. food.blog.gov.uk/2021/11/05/
the-urgency-of-eco-labelling-in-light-of-cop26/

against its direct footprint to the environment, but its effect on people – because the ultimate discussion here is: is sustainability ethical? We need to clarify whether sustainability can function ethically without neocolonialism – an ongoing system which has a direct effect on communities of colour.

I was introduced to neocolonialism by reading up on Kwame Nkrumah – a Ghanaian revolutionary and politician from the 1940s. In his book *Neocolonialism: The Last Stage of Imperialism* (*1965*), Nkrumah outlines how international monopolies still have power over African countries, showing how independence is meaningless without economic freedom. That is defined as neocolonialism – the next step of capitalism. It reveals how previously colonised lands are still controlled by the Global North – through power systems, financial debts and the guise of political collaborator. Neocolonialism in environmentalism continues the dominance of colonisers on Indigenous lands – including control over climate initiatives. The Global North are the biggest perpetrators of the climate disaster, which impacts the previously colonised lands they left behind. So this dominance feels guarded by ego rather than a solution for safety. As Nkrumah says in his book: 'Africa is having to pay a huge price once more for the historical accident that this vast and compact continent brought fabulous profits to western capitalism, first out of trade in its people and then out of imperialist exploitation.'[4] The diamond trade in Sierra Leone is a clear example of this – it is one of the poorest countries in the world and somehow is one of the most laden with diamonds and minerals. By 1937, British colonial companies unearthed one million carats annually but while Britain grew rich, the Sierra Leonean people earned almost none of this

---

4   *Neo-Colonialism The Last Stage of Imperialism*, Kwame Nkrumah. Panaf LTD, 1974.

profit. After the British left, Sierra Leone is still blocked from profiting from their own land by wealthy countries – such as the US and Japan. This control has furthered a spiral into an economical crisis; causing disease, war, poverty and child labour.

When lands were colonised by the British, they didn't bring a workforce with them – instead they used the people from that land to deplete it of its resources. They built new structures to work within: they revoked systems that enabled sustainable growth, and instead introduced capitalist growth. This was also done through the export and import of resources: extracting the people's and land's nutrition. While some celebrate the effects of the colonial power on certain lands, due to economic growth, many argue that it did nothing but strip people of the autonomy to live faithfully. The fact that the British got to choose who joined their growth, for their own benefit is nothing but harmful.

The labour of black and brown people is not something just for the history books – through neo-colonialism, the original actions from when lands were directly colonised hasn't changed the effect of the oppressor's influence. In other words, colonised and oppressed lands didn't revert to old ways of living after reaching independence. The effects remained and became the Global South's era of neo-colonialism through capitalism. That means that stolen labour remains the burden of the Indigenous, as the economical and trade powers of the Global North continued to control the land. We just need to look at modern slavery in factories around the Global South – where the authoritative power comes from the oppressors. So if we're actively allowing slave labour to continue, are we being sustainable to Earth – especially considering the slave labour is from Indigenous people.

If sustainability is environmental, economical and human,

then it's our social responsibility to confront the racial ramifications of our actions. Otherwise we are saving a planet for a bunch of privileged people to enjoy. Which in a way... perfectly describes our world right now, I suppose.

Don't get me wrong, I just ordered an oat milk latte at a coffee shop and consumed it with pleasure. There is no expectation to consume responsibly in every aspect of our lives, especially since being sustainable is within itself... unsustainable. And again, the blame comes back to us. We are considered the ones not consuming sustainably, instead of looking at the industries who aren't creating in a sustainable way. So while we beat ourselves up over this, there's only so much we can achieve within this complex system.

The need to create and care from Earth is from a deep relationship that Indigenous people have with land and nature. What is considered by many as 'Mother Earth' is in fact a gender-fluid and non-binary entity of comfort and security, and it is of colour. The 'feminine' is a value of identity that allows some to lift nature into an unreachable pedestal – something that we yearn for, mysterious and all-consuming – but not something within our grasp. The reality is that our grasp has been loosened by the grip of whiteness. By assigning a gender, it becomes folklore, a deity or mythical creature, instead of the very being of our existence.

Some people ask me how to recognise and achieve environmental ways of living, but if I'm going to be genuine, I myself do not know. I try to consume and profile certain products that are homegrown, i.e. using and paying the people of the land in a healthy manner. Although while I attempt to achieve this, I'm aware that there is some form of unethical practises leading to my enjoyment. And I absolutely do not always buy from ethical brands – I try to, but I also have put my money into the hands of those who have actively harmed land and people. While I eat plant based food, if I buy them from fast food chains, then I am adding to the carbon footprint. Does that make me a hypocrite? Maybe. But it mostly makes me human. A human attempting to survive and allow myself enjoyment.

The responsibility lies on the shoulders of the conglomerates that control our consumption, and the way in which the products are sourced. Our individual footprint is small, but it's a footprint that doesn't exist until we make it. The more we make, the more our land and people benefit. But we can't ignore the fact that substantial change is done through trade policies, governments and business reparations. They have moved the guilt onto us. 'Why don't you recycle, why do you eat meat, how can stand to buy such cheap outfits/fast fashion??'

The reality is, we can only recycle in the areas we live in, with the access we have. Meat is consumed sustainably by Indigenous people – so being vegan isn't righteous, it's simply an easier solution to unethical production. Sustainable clothing is regulated to a certain class – to those who can afford it, but wealth should not determine how economical we can be.

But there are ways that we can be sustainable, ethical, environmental: acknowledge our proximity to whiteness, privilege, and how our choices are still participating in elements of neocolonialism. Whose lands are still being stripped? Whose labour is being abused? Is whiteness still profiting from it? When I ask myself these questions, I find I'm on a more secure footing with my actions.

We can also reduce our carbon footprint, in the smallest ways. To this day, I sew up a rip, tear, or missing buttons – sometimes until the piece of clothing no longer holds together. Many of my coats have seams in pockets that expand with a scarring of thread. Holes in clothes are not a reason to discard them, or buy a new one, but instead a reason to evolve them into something personal. Avoiding adding to a capitalist and neo-colonialist structure can be done in small movements. And so, my care is now threaded into multiple coat pockets. And that care is a recognition of my mother, my grandmother, everyone before them – all consuming directly from the land, all while gently loving it.

Image description: black and white abstract illustration of shattered fragments linked by webs, the fragments showing elements of face on them.

World and Being

KANDACE SIOBHAN WALKER

...When the light reaches across the savannah and Mufasa, in Disney's *The Lion King*, tells Simba that everything in this world is interconnected.

Medicated Girls Drinking Rosé in a Rainless Heat

We have it for now, she says, but the grapes want the perfect conditions. Each summer, surpassing the last, spells less rain, overripe fruit, earlier seasons. All around her, the grass in the park is the colour of wheat. Even the historical record has topped itself.

Dehydration sets in within an hour of the sun reaching the day's full height, and the wise sweep their rubbish into carrier bags with wide, regretful arms. Where recycling bins ring with glass, the waste bins are hush with soft plastic. By morning, these objects will have gone to wherever these objects go. The plant, the sorting centre. But in a hundred years—if we aren't careful, and we aren't—all of this will still be somewhere. Not here, not in the same form, of course, but microscopic and glittering, like comet tails. All the park-leavers are aware of this destiny. The materials of the everyday are terrifying in their immortality.

Twmpa

Robin Wall Kimmerer writes, in *Braiding Sweetgrass: Indigenous Wisdom, Scientific Knowledge and the Teachings of Plants*, about the transformative power of giving somewhere a name. To name a place, she writes, is to claim it as a homeland.

This is the name of the mountain that raised her.

The Effect of Skyscapers On Birds

Varies, depending, on the skyscraper and the bird, but is relatively negligible. Just millions each year, rather than tens or hundreds of.

The smaller buildings, the modest offices and commercial spaces and two- or three-storey homes, are the big killers. The bird sees the interior rooms shielded by the glass and the bird sees the reflections in the glass, but the bird does not see the glass.

The bird never knows that the glass is there.

Maybe a window, to a bird, is a just way through a wall. For the bird, the separation is invisible. Which is why Noah is right in *The Notebook*: If a bird is a bird, then we're all birds.

Great Disaster

Translation, *maafa*. The great disaster was 1492. The great disaster was every year since. The great disaster was the extraction of people and materials. The great disaster was the violence and illness that ended the worlds of the first islands they landed on: Guanahani, Quizquella. The great disaster was the cool years, when living was easy and slaving was easier.

The great disaster was the warm years, when living was hard and slaving was harder. The great disaster was the slavers' fate. The great disaster was the slaves' fate. The great disaster was the beginning of our own extinction—all those worlds, everyday, ending.

Snake Eating its Own Tail

Eventually the world of neglect and debt will give way to a world of care and reciprocity, or a world of opportunity and obligation, as Wall Kimmerer describes it, because even as the birth of a capitalist world-relation began to de-structure ancient worlds and structure modernity, the extraction of people from the African continent to the Americas, beginning in the fifteenth century, was creating the conditions for the abolition of a system which was still, at that early juncture, nameless and uncrystallised.

Where indigenous world-relations were lost or subsumed, ecological knowledges were forced underground, and ways of knowing mutated in the dark. Wall Kimmerer argues for an acknowledgement of world's animacy, a world where human beings recognise other beings as animate, as living, and asserts that there are ways of knowing that Western science cannot accommodate. We must, she argues, find alternative and more expansive ways of structuring a world-relation that recognises the primacy of non-human intelligences and knowledges.

A widening is possible: the destruction of those ways of knowing was imperfect, sawed with a blunt edge. There is the mythological and metaphysical: the spirits, the gods, the dance. And there is the ecological and geographical: escape mapped into braids, grains of rice tucked into cornrows. The circle will be broken, the circle will be unbroken.

Failing to conjure the pure, undisturbed past, she sets about cannibalising what remains, taking what is useful. Whatever relationship to the 'natural world' she might have inherited cannot now be reclaimed wholesale, but it can be reformed out of the bones of its executioner. The immortality of the immaterial should be terrifying.

In discontinuity, always continuity.

Horse Chestnut City

Murray Bookchin, in *The Ecology of Freedom: The Emergence and Dissolution of Hierarchy*, writes that life begins with nature. He describes nature as existing in fellowship with humanity and human consciousness. This relationship goes beyond ideas of harmony and equilibrium. Nature, he writes, is as active a participant in life as we are.

A woman with a smartphone pauses beneath a tree. She asks, 'What tree is this?' and downloads an app for an answer. She's embarrassed it took her this long to ask, but until lately the city never appeared to her as being alive – except in the metaphorical sense, as a repository, a sum, of the multitudes within. But under and around and through the cracks in the concrete, of course, there is living, there is being. Even the concrete itself has its own being. And here, above her head, the tree, becoming a character in her life. Blooms shaped like whipped cream, always familiar in spring. Teardrop leaves, Madonna leaves. Conkers in the autumn, the spiky green shells. Her ignorance of its name is an inevitability of a culture built on property, on the ownership of everything. Native to the Balkan Peninsula, the app tells her. Less common in the woods where she's from but her neighbourhood in the city is silly with these trees, and very apparently in spring.

Wake Isn't the Collective Noun for a Shiver of Sharks

But it should be.

Second River Beneath That Top River

Wall Kimmerer writes that if we treat the world like it is a commodity, we will be poorer for it.

Water doesn't work this way, but when the river breaks banks for a consecutive year and begins to carry away the cars parked in the lower riverside carpark, which is being live-streamed on Facebook into a computer that all the employees are now gathering around, she thinks about the normal river beneath this sudden, violent river, a historically-rare force becoming more familiar with each year.

In Hayao Miyazaki's *Spirited Away*, the spirit of a river saves a child twice. The river spirit, trapped in a world structured by greed, has forgotten his name. And here, the original river of her childhood, that wide, kind river, that murky, polluted river, now finds itself the victim of a world upon which it cannot act, only be acted upon, an angry bull without a muleta.

The city, which loves literality, runs the rivers underground. Not like the subterranean rivers, who are autonomous, but domesticated, like a working animal. We all know the difference between the darkness we choose, and the darkness we don't. The river takes with it an entire world—the algae which requires sunlight to feed the fish which feed the birds that swim on the water's surface along the mud of the riverbank where the willows weep into the stones beat smooth and tossed out by the current where insects and arthropods hide in the crevices. When these culverted rivers are raised back up to the ground, it is called 'daylighting.' The river, returned to itself, may again become a world. So, more daylight, more worlds.

The World Keeps Ending

Clearly, the world has ended before. This is how we came to be us, here. Because if you act like you can extract people like ore, the end of the world soon come. What is a river without water? What is a village without buildings, only char and smoke? What is a people without people? These are questions she keeps asking.

Barbie Girl in a Barbie World

Even the way she learned to talk about nature betrays a great loss, an inability to figure non-human life as equal to the human. Why describe the 'natural world' as something that exists 'around' her, as if she wasn't part of it? Of course, she, and all the artificial wreckage of her life, is as much part of the natural world as a cliff face and the waves that beat it back. This is a common limitation of the language she was forced to inherit. Unlike how, as Kimmerer writes, the English language makes you a human being or an inanimate object. This is not a grammar that allows space for more life, it is a grammar of loss.

Loss is its own world. It is artificial, but transitional. Although it wishes to appear that way, it is not immutable. The generational loss of kinship with the natural world divides into separate spheres what is really a whole, shifting what we understand as living and being. But it can be shaken off, perhaps.

'Bookchin argues that the natural state of the world, and therefore of human society, is abundance. He describes a 'livingness' that walks hand-in-hand with 'knowingness'.

Which Trees Bear Fruit?

To lose a world is to lose a world-relation, the web of intimacies and interdependencies which give meaning to that world. Gradually, one is forced to forget which trees bore fruit, which plants were edible, which plants were tasty, which were poison if not cooked, which were always poison. Which animals sang which songs, which animals were curious, which animal meant a spirit was about, which animals could be used in some way—eaten or domesticated, which animals were harmless if unprovoked, which animals were deadly when trapped, which were always deadly. Which wind meant rain, which wind meant clouds of sand, which wind would break the stems of crops in two and bring down branches. Which mountains were gods in secret, which could be climbed in a day, which had treacherous ascents, which were barren, which were lush and full of rare life.

Where she grew up, the apple and pear and damson trees, and the blackberry and gooseberry bushes, bear fruit in three seasons. Winter is fruitless. The stinging nettle bore tea and pain, and the dock leaf soothed. The foxglove was poison. The mushrooms knew gods' name. The owls were percussive, the lambs were noisy and discordant, the cows were shy except at feeding. The badger wanted the sound of a snapping bone, or twig. The wind at night, in winter or early spring, meant storms, meant lost furniture, flooded bridges, telephone poles and live wires in the road, dry food, lighting paraffin candles.

Surviving the loss of a world means making legible a world which one has come to unwillingly. One must learn which trees bear fruit, which plants are edible, which plants are tasty, which are poison if not cooked, which are always poison. Which animals sing which songs, which animals are curious, which animal means a spirit is about, which animals can be used in some way—eaten or domesticated, which animals are harmless if unprovoked, which animals are deadly when trapped, which are always deadly. Which wind means rain, which wind means clouds of sand, which wind will break the stems of crops in two and bring down branches. Which mountains are gods in secret, which can be climbed in a day, which have treacherous ascents, which are barren, which are lush and full of rare life.

Video Game Moonrise

It rises like a cartoon. The midsummer moon's light is aggressive. She wakes in the night and just watches the grass, the leaves, the birds, the shadows. Objects move slower, as if the frame rate has dropped. It's like watching an old television, the black-and-white blatantly unfaithful to reality. And yet, at the same time, like a secret, like this is how the world conducts itself when none of us are looking.

The Earth Falls Apart Under the Weight of Her Own Darkness

It follows that the world which places in a hierarchy of value that which cannot be valued, in the economic sense—living beings—would be plagued by so many great disasters. Disasters that reliably find those among the world of human beings who are valued least. The flooded people, the burning people, the buried people.

And afterwards, of the silence, George Williams, the barber, said that one could hear nothing, neither the birds nor the children.

Burning Heather Smells Like Lovers

An ending is a loss, a burning away. When the gamekeepers burn the moorland's heather, the fresh growth feeds the juvenile grouse. A being exists in relation. But the burn destroys the worlds in the heather. Many beings existing in, with, for, around and because of each other, form a structure. The burn is the dissolution of living bonds in fire. The world is a relational structure. The world is being. When she was a girl in primary school, she loved the smell of burning heather, the perfume of loss. The end of the world is the loss of a structural framework, the end of an understanding. The smoke follows the prettiest girl, she says, even now, even when she knows what smoke means. The end of the world is the death of being.

Colonists Eat the Caribbean Monk Seal to Extinction

Before even naming it.

Alexis Pauline Gumbs characterises the seals as curious and without fear—the early colonists, poor at hunting, kill the monk seal for food, then, as the plantation economy solidifies, use its oil to keep the sugar cane refineries in constant motion. Seal meat and sugar, products of the death and labour of beings caught in the same machinery. Death, everywhere. By the same, short-sighted hand.

Wake of Sharks

Some say there is water without end beyond the green and flowering forests. People who appear from the treeline steal gold and grain. Buildings become ash. The ones left behind wail after the departures, and walk the long walk to the beach where they board the ships, which sail west. The gulls descend. People sink to the ocean's surface, closing their eyes against all the colour and movement and sound of the sky. Following the ships, where almost everyday waste or bodies are thrown overboard into the ocean, the sharks swallow blood and bodies.

Retreating from the ships, where almost everyday treasure or persons jump out of the ocean onto the deck, the sharks vomit blood and bodies. People float to the ocean's surface, opening their eyes to all the colour and movement and sound of the sky. The gulls fly higher and higher. Ships sail backwards, their butts swallowing the waves' white crests. People disembark on the beach and walk the long walk back home where, upon their arrival, the ones left behind shout and buildings are reconstituted from ash. People bring gold and grain, before disappearing into treeline of the green and flowering forests, beyond which some say there is water without end.

When Turner paints *The Slave Ship*, it will only be a storm, and a large, hungry fish with no name.

The Livingness

We need to re-figure our relationship to the world, Wall Kimmerer writes. We need to understand that the Earth, this world, is a gift, is sacred.

Even facing it in defiance, the events which structure her being are the events which structure and belie the nature of the world. The logics of domination and extraction stalking the centuries, the ghosts of other worlds in their wake. The stripping of people from land, of land from people, of language, knowledge, relation. It was an ecological and spiritual disfigurement. To begin to suture the wound requires a deep kinship with the world, a reciprocal relation with every being, with the livingness of it all.

Image description: black and white illustration of two feet standing on stones underwater.

I Walk, the Sea Rises

TAYLOR EDMONDS

It's May 2017 and I'm hiking along the coast of Cornwall with my partner. We've caught the bus from St Ives to Zennor to loop back on ourselves. Zennor is a small rural village on the North coast; all green fields, clifftops and stone cottages.

We start with a pint at the village pub. The kind where you have to bow your head to get through the door frame. Where there's always wood on a fire and men at the bar who don't need to order because the bartender already knows what they want. The kind of pub that makes me makes me want to step out of my body and run. But my partner is of these places. A white, Gloucestershire countryside boy who's worked in pubs his whole life, he knows their language. I watch him belong.

The coastline is a pattern of cliffs and coves, up and down. The sun beats our cheeks and the wind blocks up our noses. It's my first time on a 'proper hike' and we are ill-equipped; wearing flimsy gym trainers and carrying a small water bottle between us.

We don't know this yet, but we have accidentally taken the long route, and this walk will be three miles longer than we think. The lay of the land means that we can't see what's next until we're over a clifftop. We tell ourselves over and over that this is the last cliff, only to see the peak of another. We run out of water and arrive back with blisters, arguing over who got the route wrong and desperate for food. All of this is very overdramatic for a seven-mile walk, but we're new at this.

We clamour over rocks and watch the waves hit the coves below. The path is ours; not even a dog walker or rambler with a walking stick in sight. My partner is up ahead. I watch him stop and look out. The water is bluer here than the brown of the mudflats back home. He holds his arms wide and screams until his breath runs out. The sea is so loud I can hear only the distant bass of his voice. Then I'm screaming too, my eyes closed, wind pummelling back at me. We laugh, a proper belly-laugh like we're kids that have done something daring, and then continue with our route.

Our walk in Cornwall is the start of a love of walking in nature, after which we begin to explore Wales. I realise that I barely know the place I have lived my whole life. We climb Pen Y Fan for the highest views of Bannau Brycheiniog. We trace the coast of Pembrokeshire, where the sea is blue and the towns are small. We walk the endless muddy fields of Powys and the woodland of Hensol forest. I discover I feel true clarity in my mind and body when walking; the usual chatter of my inner thoughts becomes quiet as I focus on the next marker of the route and taking in the views. Slowly, I unlearn what I thought hiking was; double-digit mile walks and conquering mountains, the origins of which are rooted in colonialism and white supremacy.

What if hiking could be slow and unmeasurable? What if the goals of a hike weren't to tick off miles, but to familiarise yourself with the root-map of a tree? To learn the texture of moss from forest to forest?

As a teenager, all I wanted was to get out of Wales. I saw a lack of opportunity in my hometown and felt indifferent from my Welsh identity. I rarely sought out walks in nature and didn't see myself as 'outdoorsy', which felt like a trait reserved for white, middle-class families on bike rides and kayaks.

But I grew up by the sea. I've since realised that being outdoorsy is a myth that centralises the white and middle class. In my coastal town, the beach and the water are the constant backdrop. The sea is present in my most cherished family memories.

Once, researching for an audio story I was working on about the Severn Estuary, I spoke to Barry locals in the community library about their connection to the sea. People talked about the water with such familiarity and closeness, as if it was a member of their family. A woman who was unable to leave bed during a period of ill health, told me how the view of the sea from her window brought her inner peace and got her through recovery.

I relate to this treasuring of the landscape. I've chased the incoming tide across the pebbled coastline at night, sunbathed on the sand with my late great-grandparents, spent the whole day walking the coast and cooled off in the muddy water. I have always sought out the sea to bring me a sense of tranquillity. Even just the sight of it from a distance makes me breathe better.

The women in my family rarely go out in nature alone, and never dare to break the unwritten rulebook of *How to Not Get Yourself Murdered*. Without ever really talking about it, I learned that exploring outside beyond a trip to the shops or a walk in a familiar, populated area was just too risky, and not something we did.

Like many women and femme-presenting people, I am terrified of what can happen to me on a walk. I was taught to be home before dark, always stick to busy roads, and keep one headphone out with the sharp edge of my keys ready between my fingers. I've had my path blocked, my arm dragged toward a waiting taxi, been followed, ass grabbed, taunted. These experiences have felt so unremarkable and part of life, I have even counted myself lucky. Meanwhile, the news cycle is overwhelmed with reports of another woman murdered on a walk home. Each time I feel grief for a life cut short. It is not irrational to think that it could someday be me, my daughter, or best friend. Hyper-awareness of this meant that on all of my walks and discoveries across Wales, I was never alone. With my partner I felt safe, my risk reduced by his presence. It is hard to take up space in nature when governed by a fear of it. Yet I started to resent the fact I felt like I couldn't travel and seek these places for myself alone, when my partner could so easily.

As I grappled with my personal desires and fears about nature, my work increasingly engaged with the threats of climate change. In 2021-2022, I was appointed as Poet-in-Residence for the Future Generations Commissioner for Wales. A very lengthy title for a unique opportunity. My role was a result of the Well-being of Future Generations Act (2015), the first law of its kind in the world. It requires public bodies in Wales to think about the long-term impact of their decisions on future generations, and to make decisions that work towards a better future for the well-being of people yet to be born.

As Poet-in-Residence, I was challenged with creatively communicating the act and its causes, offering a more accessible, evocative creative form that could humanise stories and sit alongside statistics and jargon-heavy reports. I was used to deep dives of research on Google to support my poems, but now I had access to researchers and experts to fill the gaps in my knowledge. Throughout the year, I wrote commissions to accompany new research on Universal Basic Income and future inequality, worked with communities that suffered from flooding and told the story of what Wales was trying to do on a global stage at COP26. Prior to the role, my poetry hadn't reached much further than poetry magazines or literary circles, so to see the potential of my work creating an impact on topics that were important to me was both incredible and overwhelming.

A map released in 2021, based on research by Natural Resources Wales, predicted the impact of climate change in Wales, with many areas at risk from rising sea levels and increased flooding by 2050. The map of my town, Barry, is illuminated in green and blue, showing the majority of the coast and inland docks area are threatened.

When I first saw the maps, I was on a train from Edinburgh to Aberdeen with my mum, nan and great aunties. A scenic journey that crosses Forth Bridge over the Firth of Forth Estuary, perfectly dramatic with low fog and misty rain. I had joined them on their annual trip to my great-grandmother's homeland, wanting to connect with the woman who despite passing when I was a child, has had a huge impact on my life. We spent grey days tracing her steps. I saw the street she grew up in, the big door of her old terraced house. I tasted a Buttery for the first time; an Aberdeen special of flaky, butter-soaked pastry.

The trip felt so significant, like something I had been waiting to do without knowing it yet, to connect to her better. My mind was drawn back to those maps. Would my potential great-grandchild would be able to trace my routes around my hometown in the same way I had traced my great-grand-mothers? Would they be able to sit on the wall of the Old Harbour pier, legs dangling over the receding tide, where I had heady conversations with friends about the lives we would have when we grew up? Would they be able to cross the jagged rocks of Friars Point to the secret spot where I had my first kiss with a girl I loved?

Soon after, I wrote the first poem of my residency, *My Magnolia Tree*. The poem imagines a narrator that learns about her late grandmother's life through letters she had written to her before her passing. The grandmother's town is lost to floods, and as a result, the granddaughter doesn't get to see the magnolia tree that her grandmother planted for her. She aches for a place that no longer exists.

Through my writing and community work, I developed a deeper sense of belonging in Wales through my connection with nature. The place I once couldn't wait to leave became unimaginable to live without. I understood better the impact of nature on the well-being of myself and others, and how art had a unique ability to communicate this in ways that connected me with others. Yet, I still felt afraid to walk in nature alone.

After *My Magnolia Tree* was published in a video performance, people commented on how emotive the poem was, that they didn't realise how imminent the impacts of climate change could be felt on their doorstep. The poem was a gateway for them to go on and read further about the issue of climate change, the impact of which is happening already in places such as Pakistan and Fiji, as millions of people are displaced from their ancestral villages.

In Welsh Legend, Cantre'r Gwaelod was a sunken ancient kingdom believed to be underwater in what is now Cardigan Bay. There are multiple versions of the myth, and in the most recent, its low-lying land was protected from the sea by a dyke and floodgates. Through negligence, one of the gates was left open, and the land was swallowed by the sea at high tide. Sightings of the remnants of Cantre'r Gwaelod have been reported over the years, with recent revelations connecting the place to a sunken forest at Ynsylas. During storms, the stumps of the forests' oak, birch, and pine trees have been spotted, as well as human footprints preserved in hardened peat. It's said that on a quiet night, the church bells of Cantre'r Gwaelod can be heard, ringing from under the water in warning.

After my residency, I felt tired of making myself small, of hiding, of fear. Emboldened with the knowledge of my experiences, I realised that I deserve a connection with nature just as much as anyone else. I decide to hike alone. I am consumed by all the ways I will die, the ways I will be followed. The way I'll cross a man's path and avoid his eyes, or hear his footsteps behind me quicken. The way he'll talk to me, grab at me, look at me. If anything was to happen, certainly people will ask why I was out hiking alone, risking my safety.

Despite my anxieties, I move forward. I plan my first solo walk along the coast. The familiar openness makes it feel safer. The route is a nine-mile loop from my flat. First, along roads, then to the coast, up through a stretch of woodland then back to the pebbles until I join the clifftop coastal path for my last mile home. I pack water, lunch, my camera, a journal and my phone. I take precautions. My partner knows my route and ETA, I take a route that starts from home so he can get to me quickly if I need him. I nervously check the tidal range for the fifth time.

On the day, the weather is typically Welsh, the sky brooding with moody clouds and drizzle. But I hold out hope for sun breaks. I wear my walking boots, leggings, layer up T-shirts and a long sleeve over a waterproof jacket. It's late March, and it feels like we are beginning to emerge from the longest winter. Houses are lined with rows of daffodils, trees boast magnolia. The scent of it tickles my nose.

I've always been a daydreamer. People describe me as someone who lives in my head 'away with the fairies'. I'm conscious that being this way lends itself to creativity and writing, but I struggle to be present. I lose big chunks of time in anxious thoughts and imagined scenarios, only half in reality. It's when I'm walking that I feel most present. With so much to observe and take note of, and a route to focus on, I am pulled to the present. I indulge in it.

Emerging from my town to the A-roads, a few cars pass by but it's mostly just me. Very quickly, the day-to-day anxieties and worries that I wake up with, begin to quiet. As I focus on my next waypoint, *left at the end of this road, cross at the junction,* my mind clears.

As I'm making my way down a grassy hill, I get my first sight of the sea. When I imagined this walk, I wanted the reflection of the glittering sun and heat on my cheeks. But even in the moody-grey sky, the mud-tinted water, the sight of it spurs something in me. I climb down to the coast, onto layers of big, flat rocks littered with pools. I spot tiny, translucent crabs in the water. Thick lines of slick seaweed drape over the rocks, wet from the residing tide.

On my course along the coast, the rocks become small and bulky, stacked on top of each other with deep gaps between them, so I need to keep my eyes on my feet. I pass a few dog walkers who smile and nod at me. Then another woman about my age, also walking alone in the opposite direction. I wonder if it took as much for her to do this as it did for me.

Next up, I fork off from the beach and up a small opening into a patch of woodland. There's an abandoned building ruin left to rot, covered in fading graffiti and half-standing. Strings of vines have cut through the rocks, surviving, taking back.

The woodland feels like a different world from the openness of the coast. The trees bend and enclose me, blocking the light. Birds flitter between branches and fill the space with birdsong. The path becomes muddy, caking my boots. I take a sharp incline and trail along the edge of a cliff. My heartbeat quickens, my body feels hot and energised with the work. From here, between the trees, I can see the beach below and hear the distant sea, look over to the other side of the Bristol Channel towards Weston Super Mare. I'm now two-thirds into my journey, and my legs ache. I stop for lunch, journal, and call my partner with this view.

Afterwards I feel refreshed, and the path takes me back down onto the beach, with some clamouring down unstable rocks. From here on out it's easy, I follow the line of the coast until I can see my town.

When I get to the end of my route, the tide is rolling in, and I stop to watch it, cupping the foam of it in my hands. I take off my shoes and socks to walk along the edge of the water, the cold winding me as it reaches my feet. The pebbles hurt, but I don't care. I'm thinking of being five or six, at this beach with my great-grandparents. Watching my grandmother, waves rushing at her feet, holding out her arms for balance.

After my first solo hike, I thought that I'd feel some sort of change within me as a result. As if I would transform into someone braver, who stood in the face of fear. In reality, it feels natural, unremarkable, like something I have done many times before. Instead, I have relaxed into the feeling of knowing I walk alone again and again, forging a connection with the landscape. I have always been sure that one day I will have a daughter. I'll teach her to carve her own stories along the coast, to be brave in quiet ways. I wonder how different this view will look then; if she will be able to walk this trail, or if it will be lost to the rising sea.

Image description: black and white illustration of a smiling woman with long dark hair, her body wrapped in vines and leaves.

Flowerpots

DURRE SHAHWAR

There's a picture of me standing above Llyn y Fan Fach 'little lake near the peak' in 2017, tall and triumphant, my black hair dipped in blonde billowing in the wind, with my back to the camera. Llyn a Fan Fach is located in the Western Bannau Brycheiniog (Brecon Beacons National Park). The lake is surrounded by several mountain peaks. In the picture, I'm looking down at the almost black lake in front of me, as though recreating Caspar David Friendreich's painting *Wanderer Above the Sea of Fog* (1818). It was one of the first paintings I learnt about while studying art in college, instantly mesmerised by the Romanticism movement and specifically its focus on the symbiosis between humans and landscapes that evoke in us feelings of awe, wonder, terror, and peace all at once. The hike had been a spontaneous one with friends. We had packed very little snacks and water. Despite it being summer, the day had been overcast with a light drizzle and a cool breeze which made me glad I had packed a parka as an extra layer. We had arrived at twelve noon with determination to climb the steep mountain from the bottom all the way to the top. I remember marvelling at the way that my then underweight twenty-something body with little sleep the night before could push through and keep pushing beyond tiredness and fatigue to get to the top. The excitement of being in a space that was 'wild' and had to be overcome drove me. Each step revealed a new crag or a trickle of water that surprised me, while in the distance, white dots of cattle speckled the magnificent sloping green mountains.

There are more pictures like these accumulated over the years: me standing on a slippery rock in front of a beautifully cascading waterfall at the Four Waterfalls Walk, near Ystradfellte, Brecon. Me looking down from up above while hiking on a narrow and dangerous path by the side of a mountain that I wouldn't want to slip on. Me as a young child watching my sister float in a shallow pool of water in Murree, Pakistan. Me as I stand looking across the stretch of white sand, mountains, and sky-blue seas at Rhossilli bay. Me looking out at the horizon while walking the coastal path that connects Caswell and Langland Bay. Many of these pictures often containing the same pose of a triumphant brown woman looking away from the camera, comfortable and at ease with her body amidst breathtaking and powerful landscapes.

Scrolling through pictures of me with friends in 'the great outdoors' and the longing to return to them kept me going in July 2022, when I was bed-ridden for most of the day after a severe stomach virus, which I had ignored the signs of for two weeks. I had put the symptoms that I had been feeling down to simply being a little bit exhausted from work and life. But ignoring this meant I ended up in A&E at five am because my body was so depleted that it struggled with even keeping down water. I was put on multiple bags of IV fluids and medications as I sat shaking and shivering (despite it being July) before I was sent home with instructions that I'll probably be okay and back to 'normal' in a few weeks. But weeks turned into months. Months in which I dealt with other health issues and was forced to confront how burnt out I was and to reconsider my relationship with myself and nature. I was forced to ask myself what it means to love nature from the safety boundary of my home. When I returned home from the hospital, one of my oldest friends sent me peace lilies with the note: 'I hope this plant becomes a reminder to look after yourself like you would this plant.'

Until that point, my relationship had varied between excursions in local parks and green spaces to mountains and forests. The former places were safe, 'easy'. The mountains and forests that I got lost within were exciting and made me push past my 'high-functioning' anxiety to be in their presence. Many of us are often drawn to the untameable and thrilling aspects of the natural word. Traditional narratives of how we approach nature have also been shaped by ideas of 'conquering' or 'overcoming' nature and the unknown that also shaped my relationship to it. It was the same relationship that I had with many other aspects in my life – of pushing hard and beyond my limits because I didn't want to be held back by my class, gender, background, skin colour, mental health. Everyday metaphors of 'moving mountains' and 'climbing mountains' that create measurements of our effort and success also fed into this narrative. As admirable an endeavour as they are, they still speak to an ableist and colonialist way of approaching the landscape. It would be simplistic to say that it is the sole reason I was drawn to extreme and beautiful landscapes, as I also feel immense joy being in them. But along with the joy was also a desire to stand on a high peak and feel accomplished. To prove something.

But in the summer of 2022, being forced to be still in a way that not even COVID lockdowns had, made me confront what it means to have a relationship with nature when ill health and burnout means you can't access these landscapes. When we were in lockdown, I was aware that that this imposed stillness was external. When sick, my body felt more fragile than before, and the stillness was internal. Even as my stomach healed, and I began to eat regular meals again, I was fatigued, with brain fog, palpitations, and little stamina for many months afterwards. My anxiety developed into agoraphobia because my symptoms were so unpredictable. I was no longer faced with the uncertainty of the world, but also with the uncertainty of my body within it, and it was no longer something I could push past. Due to this, my relationship with nature deepened in a way that it hadn't when hiking and standing on slippery rocks in front of waterfalls.

There aren't any pictures of this, but I have memories of me playing in the rain on the first-floor terrace of our house in Pakistan as a child. I remember the water pooling around my ankles as I splashed across the terrace, my clothes soaked down to my skin while my mum stood and watched over me from the window. It was a moment of pure joy after days of scorching heat. Twenty different plants lined the walls of our terrace. My parents had taught us to water and look after them all year long, but especially in humid South Asian summers. After the rain, their leaves were a perky, bright, rich green. They were joyous as I was. In summer 2022, I remind myself of this memory as I tend to the peace lilies my friend gave me, but also to the roses, hydrangeas, wildflowers, lavender, pansies, green chillis, tomatoes, and mint we grew in the concrete garden of our council house. A garden that had been ruthlessly cemented over by the previous owner. A garden that I had once detested because I thought that nothing beautiful and green could grow there.

I spend the summer taking pictures of flowerpots and the way their shadows fall in the sunlight onto the cemented ground below, somehow making it beautiful, to remind myself of the gentleness, care, and the journey to their growth even after they're long gone in the winter. I remind myself that nature exists even here. I remind myself of how it can be known and unknown even in small ways; I can predict when a planted seed might bloom, but I can't always control when a leaf will turn yellow and fall because of heat or overwatering. I can only try. And despite the knowledge that nature can be volatile; that storms can break houses and seas can drown people; I hold onto the gentle stillness that the flowerpots remind me to incorporate into my life. I remind myself of the time they take to bloom, and how the process itself is precarious and fragile. That for it to push through the soil and emerge at the top defiantly is still as fierce as a mountain peak. That this seemingly small and simple act is as much worth celebrating as hiking up mountains is. In doing so, I'm led to a deeper knowing of my body and its capacities and needs too. I learn to be gentler and more patient with the time it takes me to do small things; of the healing that is occurring underneath even if I cannot see it.

In recent years, there's been a lot of writing that approaches nature as a source of healing, and alongside it, criticism of this being cliché or reductive to what nature does for us. In response to this, I find myself asking who gets to define what nature is and what it does for us – who gets to access it for healing, who gets to write or create art about it? As inspiring as the Romanticists were, they weren't without their faults, one being the incredibly Western lens through which they depicted nature when Sufi poets and artists in the East were talking about the majesty of nature centuries before. So many Sufi poems and music emphasise the inner sense of peace that can be found within nature from simple acts, as opposed to the more extremes. It is this way of thinking that I found myself embracing in summer 2022.

It isn't that tending to the flowerpots healed me. Healing required rebuilding my mind-body connection and using all the tools at my disposal, from yoga to a better diet, changing my working and creative practices, therapy, support, and tests from doctors that told me I AM OKAY. But tending to the flowerpots amongst all this reminded me to be where I am at. To embrace it, rather than yearn restlessly to be elsewhere, whether it be literal landscapes or metaphorical ones. As a brown woman who carries the history of colonial violence, and who has experienced state violence, my burnout and illness were a reminder that I can't spend my life achieving and conquering in every area of my life to prove my worth. That gentleness and slowness which is present within nature is a decolonised way of living and creating that I needed to incorporate into my life. Not narratives of conquering when access to many outdoor spaces is still limited for people who have visible and unseen disabilities and illnesses.

All of this also served as a reminder of how important photographs, visual art, and writing are as tools for cultural memory and history and how they allow us to autonomously construct narratives of the self. We are all aware that historically, people of colour have either been washed out of these modes of creating or have been the subject of a white gaze. Picking up a camera or a pen to capture our relationship to nature is a way to challenge as well as celebrate our lives. In that act, we are saying: this matters. I matter. Bear witness. The pictures I have accumulated over the years kept me going in Summer 2022, but a year later I'm feeling braver than ever and dreaming of landscapes that I can walk or hike gently and slowly within. And of course, take pictures.

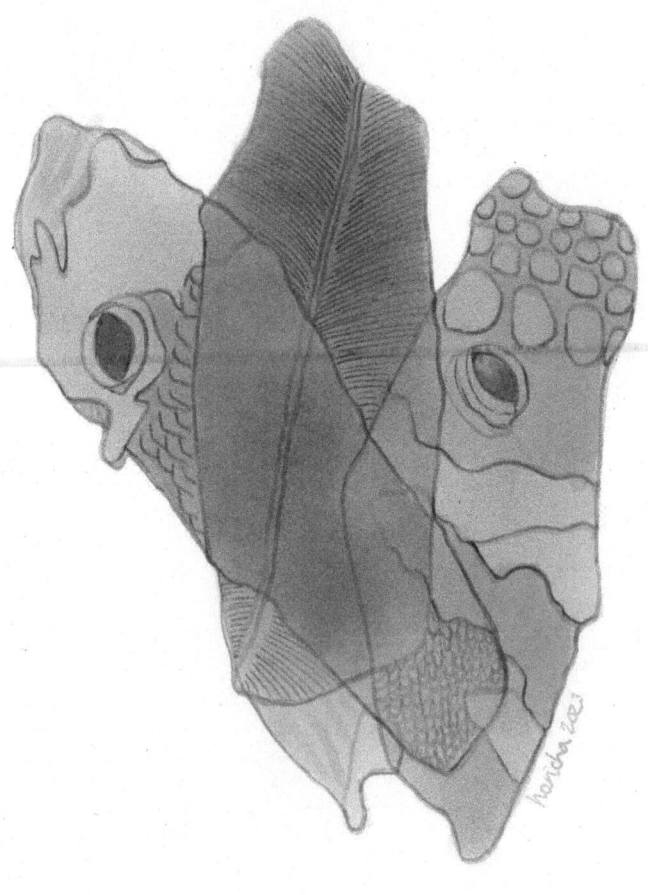

Image description: black and white abstract illustration of fragments showing elements of tropical leaves, lizards and frogs.

Nature

A Recollection, A Reclamation

ADÉ̩OLÁ DEWIS

A prayer to *Ile* (Mother Earth) starts with the acknowledgement that we are from the earth and that it is to the earth that we inevitably return.

Ifa – the Yoruba belief system, teaches that we are nature. As above, so below. What is outside is also inside.

We are aware of the residual fear or discomfort of the sea and of working on the land, that some of us carry due to the trauma of our transatlantic journeys – and the deeply embedded legacies of the colonial project.

What follows is a story of recollection, a memory in fragments that feeds a cyclical dance back to myself.

I grew up in Trinidad. As children, my sisters and I were surrounded by nature. Despite the house geckos, home provided some shelter from the creatures of the outside world. We were encouraged to be indoors during the hottest time of the day. We would dance in the rain when the season changed from dry, to rainy. The climate encouraged usual tropical intruders to venture indoors such as cockroaches, mosquitoes, flies and spiders. Occasionally we would have a large *zandolee* (ground

lizard) scamper in, a lost, confused bird, bat or *crapaux* (toad).
These unexpected encounters with creatures of the outdoors
usually resulted in the type of high-pitched scream that audibly
translated to the insistence that the now terrified creature be
escorted back to its outdoor oasis by our father (or anyone
brave enough to coax or handle the animal). Outdoors, in
nature, we knew we were in *their* home. It was a place of play,
of fear, of adventure and of freedom. In our childhood world,
nature was the *backyard*, the *beach* and the *bush*.

The Backyard
Our house was in a residential area, on a street with many
other houses – each with their own unique architecture
and surrounding yard. Our yard had many varieties of trees
including mango, avocado and cherry. I remember the gravelled
driveway and the plants – like aloe and lime, around the rich
earth. This was a place of play and adventure. I don't remember
if we climbed the trees – there were camouflaged lizards on
the barks and leaves and unintentionally touching one was
not a desirable thought. There were also colourful birds – the
Kiskadee with their yellow breast, that we recited a poem about
in school, and the hummingbirds. Sometimes we could glimpse
the bright green of an iguana high up in a tall coconut tree.
The yard had its own magic and it transformed in many ways:
from daytime to night, on a sunny day or rainy day, or when
the fruits were in season, ripe and falling to the ground, some
devoured to the seed by birds.

There were other parts to our yard that were darker, damp,
and seemed, through little girl eyes, to be scary. I remember
an area that grew a plant called *dasheen*. This leafy dark green
bush was nourished by wet muddy ground in shaded areas.
The thing about wet, muddy ground is that it is the ideal
habitat for frogs and *crapaux*. There were *crapaux* under rocks

and *crapaux* looking like rocks. Our irrational fear of these amphibious lifeforms stemmed from the sheer prevalence of them. We were taught that some were poisonous. Our dogs would get frothy drool if they bit one. Boys in school would catch them and chase the girls. And in our yard, they ate our dog food – we would feed our dogs in the evening, only to be greeted by a very large, very full *crapaux* that had relieved our pets of their leftovers, slowly hopping out of the dog bowl.

My father once sent me into the yard to cut an aloe leaf. I remember being irritated and annoyed and cutting the leaf with that irritation. Days later I found the entire plant dead.

The prevalence of fruit trees in our yard meant that at night we would sometimes be woken by intruders in our trees collecting fruit. Sometimes this was harmless enough. Sometimes they would poison our dogs. Sometimes, my father would be outside under the stars, blazoning his *cutlass* (machete) to a man in the tree. Sometimes the police got involved. I recall one man in our tree shouting to our father 'this is *Jah* land, this is *Jah* tree'– the yard at night reminded us of our privilege and our vulnerability.

The Beach

Our father is an excellent swimmer. He would swim far, far out and we would anxiously keep an eye on his head along the horizon, until he was safely back to the shore. Our mother spent most of her childhood in St Vincent and Grenada where the beach was a part of her daily ritual. We went to the beach often but getting there was a family outing, an expedition. Although we lived on an island, the terrain was mountainous and so getting to the beach was a long drive – winding roads, going up, to then go down. My sisters and I would see the glistening of the sun-kissed sea water in the approaching distance and know that it was not that beach at which we would be stopping. We would have to get to the other one. We always wanted to go to the nearest one but on reaching the third, sometimes fourth beach along our drive, we appreciated the winding, and the nauseating journey that got us there. The destination was cleaner, not so busy, worth the wait and nicer somehow. Roadside vendors sold pickled seasoned fruit (*chow*) and watermelon in giant slices. The sand was often a little too hot. My father and I engaged in a ritual of running the length of the beach – bare feet, cooled by the water along the shoreline. On our run back we would see my mother and sisters in the far distance, gradually getting closer.

The beach held the potency of a threshold. It was a liminal space – shifting and changing, full of energy, rejuvenating and healing. For me, the edge of the world.

I remember visiting Trinidad when my firstborn was a toddler. We made the familiar journey to a beach. After spending some time playing by the shore, he excitedly ran towards me saying 'Mummy, the sea listens to me' – he recounted that the waves went forward and back when he asked. I said that was a very special gift, to hold it close and remember it. On our next visit a couple years later (and to that beach) he said the sea no longer listened to him. I saw him standing in authority, commanding the waves with instructions. He held the connection close and did remember – but on this day, the connection was misplaced. I shared that we are not the masters of the sea. When we see ourselves as part of it (as he did when he was younger) we're able to flow with it, to see our interconnectedness – have a conversation.

My sister and I nearly drowned as children. We were at a beach with our father, his sisters, and his parents. We were playing in the shallow water. The seabed was uneven and without warning we were suddenly underwater, unable to find our footing. In our scramble for air, we were unsuccessfully pushing down on each other, in order to get our head above water. Our father got us to safety.

Sea water tastes horrible. It is full of life and death. We feel the small fishes swim past our bare legs. We are told to avoid periods when the jellyfish are abundant. We see the fishermen and a stingray – we learn to navigate this water that is healing, cleansing, sustaining and a reminder of journeys. Tumbled by powerful waves we still know we have restless ancestors in those ocean graves.

On some days we carry fruit and make an offering of thanksgiving to the sea.

The Bush

On our drives outside of the city, we would be framed on both sides of the road by lush, dense forests. Trinidad is beautifully green, with wild rainforests. The *bush* in my memory was a place of folklore, of magic, of ritual and mystery, medicines and healing. In our lingo, *the bush* also signified rural living spaces or *country*. Here, I use *bush* to refer to forests.

We went to the *bush* a couple of times, usually to find a river or a waterfall.

I remember my father taking me, my then-husband and our new baby to the *bush*. We parked by the side of a road and he asked us to leave our shoes in the car. We walked through narrow, barely visible man made paths. The earth was damp underfoot. Eventually we came to a river, shaded by the forest trees – the water ran gently along rocks and pebbles, creating a dreamlike oasis. The water was calm and we could sense there was so much life around us. My father gave my husband a *cutlass* and disappeared for a bit. By the time he returned, it was starting to get dark.

The setting of the sun meant the awakening of the life around us. I kept my gaze forward, held tightly to baby and by stepping steadily on the damp earth, allowed the multiple forest frogs to hop away from our path back to the car.

Away from the noise and pollution of the city, Trinidad's rich folklore dwells within the *bush*.

On our night-time drives, hugged by a showreel of rainforest trees, we would have our eyes peeled in the hope of glimpsing *Papa Bois* (Father of the Forest) with his form half beast, half man; or a supernatural lost bride, crossing the street in search of her betrothed. Our folklore teaches morals, often using fear to encourage children to make choices that were kind to nature or their community. Sometimes the folklore characters and narratives were just scary – we put salt on our windowsills in case a *Soucouyant* (a blood-sucking 'witch') were to visit.

I've read of the *bush* as a place for nocturnal gatherings, for talking drums in the hills, for maroon communities and the planning of the Haitian revolution.

How do we remember what we forgot to remember?

We know we are nature – from the earth we come and to the earth we return. Andre Tanker sang that we are the earth and the fire. Science shows us that we too are stardust – composed of the same matter. In recalling these fragments of memory from my childhood, I know that I am re-membering fragments of Trinidad in my new landscape in Wales. In the Welsh landscape, I walk in the grass when given a choice, I pause and touch the barks of city trees, I close my eyes and face the sun in the summer weeks, affirming that rain is a blessing and the wind, a reminder of life's breath. (I have encountered fewer frogs here). I tell myself that I belong in this environment, can be nurtured by it, just as by any other natural space. The beaches here are beautiful – often cold.

My spirit yearns for the warmth of home.

I am seeding an understanding of how nature feeds us – the sun, rain, wind, bush, beach, backyard and interaction with creatures. I am seeding an understanding of what this *feeding* means for our own body, to exist and thrive best in different spaces and with other bodies – the ways in which sitting on the concrete slabs in my backyard in Cardiff during the summer months allows me to recognize the same sun as nourishing and the cool breeze as breath, connecting me to this land and all land. The unconscious connection we had with nature as children, playing barefoot in the backyard, is here, being newly recalled through deliberate gestures that aim to intentionally connect us, again.

These ritual gestures make real, a way of understanding ourselves, invoking the transformational magic of backyard harvests, the power of in-between, liminal shorelines, the creative imagination, and the possibility of the dark and unknown.

Acknowledgements

We want to thank the remarkable writers for trusting us with their words and their voices which grace this anthology and for coming on a journey with us to create something unique together. Your contributions have enriched our lives, broadened our horizons, and left an indelible mark on the literary legacy of nature writing. We want to thank 404 Ink for understanding our vision for the book. We want to thank Books Council of Wales for giving it the support that it needed from its very inception so that an idea could be turned into reality and Creative Scotland who provided further support. We also want to thank everyone who has supported this book in whatever format.

– Durre Shahwar &
Nasia Sarwar-Skuse

Contributor Biographies

Adéọlá Dewis – Trinidadian artist whose work engages transformation, diaspora and performances of fragments. She is founder of Laku Neg, an artist run company interested in African diaspora knowledge exchange.

Alycia Pirmohamed – co-founder of the Scottish BPOC Writers Network, co-organiser of the Ledbury Poetry Critics Programme and author of *Another Way to Split Water*, short-listed for the Raymond Souster Award 2023, longlisted for the Laurel Prize and the Jhalak Prize 2023. Her essay collection *A Beautiful and Vital Place* won the 2023 Nan Shepherd Prize.

Durre Shahwar – writer and an AHRC PhD Candidate in Creative Writing, researching autofiction, language, and identity at Cardiff University, where she also teaches. As well as *Gathering*, she is the co-editor of *Just So You Know* (Parthian Books). Her work has been published widely, including *Wasafiri Magazine*, where she has been a Writer-in-Residence. She is a Future Wales Fellow, undertaking creative research around climate justice through art. Durre is currently working on her debut non-fiction book, a sample of which was shortlisted and highly commended for the Morley Lit Prize. Durre is repped by Nelle Andrew at Rachel Mills Literary Agency. Durreshahwar.com

Hanan Issa – current National Poet of Wales and prolific writer, poet and artist whose debut pamphlet *My Body Can House Two Hearts* was published by Burning Eye Books.

Jasmine Isa Qureshi (they/she) – follows the path of a writer, a naturalist, and a storyteller. A journalist (penning articles for a large variety of magazines, e-journals and blogs, from *Gay Times* and *Gal-Dem* to *Birdwatch* and *BBC Wildlife*), a wildlife television/media researcher – previously working at Wild Space Productions on a series for Netflix, BBC Natural History Unit / BBC Earth, and Sound Off Films, a freelance wildlife film-maker, an Ambassador for the Bumblebee Conservation Trust, the Engagement Officer for the youth-led organisation A Focus On Nature, an advisor for RSPB England, an activist, a marine biologist, a poet and a speaker and consultant, she finds the links between her many worlds as an intersectional queer ecologist and writer.

Kandace Siobhan Walker – writer and artist. Her debut pamphlet, *Kaleido*, was published by Bad Betty Press in 2022. Her first collection, *Cowboy*, was published by CHEERIO in 2023.

Katherine Cleaver – neurodiverse disabled Anglo-Indian writer finishing her PhD with Swansea University. In 2019 she was long listed in the New Welsh Writers Award and has had a memoir published by Parthian in *Just So You Know* and by Honno in *Painting the Beauty Queens Orange*. In 2022 she was published in *Land of Change: stories of struggle and solidarity from Wales* and in 2023 she gained a highly commended for 'The King of Swansea' by the New Welsh Writers Award. She has been published in the *New Welsh Reader* and writes a monthly column for Nation Cymru.

Khairani Barokka – Minang-Javanese writer and artist, and Editor of *Modern Poetry in Translation*. Her work has been presented widely internationally, and aims to centre disability justice as anticolonial praxis. Okka's latest book, *Ultimatum Orangutan* (Nine Arches), was shortlisted for the Barbellion Prize.

Louisa Adjoa Parker – writer, poet, and consultant on anti-racism, and equity, diversity and inclusion. She is of English-Ghanaian heritage and based in the southwest. Her books include *How to wear a skin* (Indigo Dreams), *Stay with me* (Colenso Books), and *She can still sing* (Flipped Eye). She has a memoir forthcoming with Little Toller Books.

Maya Chowdhry – writer and multidisciplinary artist. Her poetry collections include *The Seamstress and the Global Garment* (Crocus) and *Fossil* (Peepal Tree Press). She was artist in residence for the Critical Poetics Summer School with Nottingham Trent University.

Nadia Javed – Nadia Javed, is a British Muslim of Indian/Pakistani heritage, a punk musician, actor, activist, and writer from Hayes, Middlesex. Notable as the frontwoman of the feminist band The Tuts. She toured with Kate Nash, The Selecter, The Specials and performed at Glastonbury's leftfield stage. Her music been featured on BBC 6 Music, Radio one and Radio X.

Sharan Dhaliwal – founder the UK's leading South Asian culture magazine *Burnt Roti* and author of debut non-fiction *Burning My Roti* (Hardie Grant). She is the Director of Middlesex Pride and was on the list of global influential women for the BBC 100 Women 2019.

Dr Sofia Rehman – independent scholar specialising in Islam and Gender. She works as a knowledge building consultant for Musawah Movement and as a PhD candidate she was a PG Impact Fellow at the Centre of Religion and Public Life and PRHS Scholar. She is founder of the Islam and Gender read alongs & is the author of a Treasury of Aisha bint Abu Bakr (Kube publishing) and the forthcoming monograph, *Gendering the Hadith: Recentering the Authority of Aisha, Mother of the Believers* (Oxford University Press).

Susmita Bhattacharya – Indian-born writer whose debut novel, *The Normal State of Mind* (Parthian) was long-listed at the Mumbai Film Festival, 2018. Her short story collection, *Table Manners* (Dahlia Publishing) won the Saboteur Award for Best Short Story Collection and was a finalist for the Hall & Woodhouse DLF Prize. She received funding from Arts Council England in 2021 to write a radio drama and is a mentor for underrepresented writers.

Taylor Edmonds – poet, writer and creative facilitator from South Wales and author of debut poetry pamphlet *Back Teeth* (Broken Sleep Books). Taylor was the 21-22 Poet in Residence for the Future Generations Commissioner for Wales and has received a Rising Star award from Literature Wales and Firefly Press. Taylor is currently working on her first YA novel.

Tina Pasotra – artist, writer, director and filmmaker, whose interdisciplinary practice bridges moving image, theatre, sound, dance, installation and architecture. Credits include films and projects 'I Choose' (2020), nominated for Best Short Film BAFTA Cymru 2021, 'But Where Are You From?' (2017) and 'Sisters' (2018) at National Theatre Wales. Since 2019, Tina has been developing a series of creative interventions in collaboration with the National Botanic Garden of Wales, most recently creating a residency project called 'Mycelium' at the gardens, supported by Arts Council Wales. Tina is currently a writer in residence with Five Acts developing an original TV Pilot.

Editor Biographies

Durre Shahwar is a writer and an AHRC PhD Candidate in Creative Writing, researching autofiction, language, and identity at Cardiff University, where she also teaches. As well as *Gathering*, she is the co-editor of *Just So You Know* (Parthian Books). Her work has been published widely, including *Wasafiri Magazine*, where she has been a Writer-in-Residence. She is a Future Wales Fellow, undertaking creative research around climate justice through art. Durre is currently working on her debut non-fiction book, a sample of which was shortlisted and highly commended for the Morley Lit Prize. Durre is repped by Nelle Andrew at Rachel Mills Literary Agency. Durreshahwar.com

Nasia Sarwar-Skuse is a solicitor and an award-winning writer of the Queen Mary Wasafiri New Writing Prize (2023). She is undertaking a PhD in Creative Writing at Swansea University, researching colonialism, migration, and their intersections with individual and material memory. As a Creative Writing facilitator, Nasia conducts workshops within the community and, more recently, at Ty Newydd Writing Centre of Wales.

In 2022, Nasia was commissioned by Literature Wales and Natural Resource Wales to co-lead a nature project, engaging women of colour through creative writing workshops and storytelling, with the goal of fostering a sense of belonging and reclaiming their space in the environment. She is passionate about the presence of authenticity in literature by ethnic voices and its intersections with diaspora and gender. Nasia is currently working as a lead artist on a decolonisation project, and writing has appeared in several publications.

Illustrator Biography

Haricha Abdaal is a British Indian illustrator, translator and publishing assistant at Honford Star.
harichaart.com